AFRICAN THEOLOGY IN ITS SOCIAL CONTEXT

Bénézet Bujo

Translated from the German by
John O'Donohue, M. Afr.

Wipf & Stock
PUBLISHERS
Eugene, Oregon

Wipf and Stock Publishers
199 W 8th Ave, Suite 3
Eugene, OR 97401

African Theology in Its Social Context
By Bujo, Bénézet
Copyright©1992 Orbis Books
ISBN: 1-59752-616-9
Publication date 3/29/2006
Previously published by Orbis Books, 1992

Original language edition, Afrikanische Theologie
in ihrem gesellschaftlichen Kontext, published by
Patmos Verlag GmbH, 1986

Original title: *Afrikanische Theologie in ihrem gesellschaftlichen Kontext* by Patmos
Verlag GmbH, Düsseldorf, Germany, 1986

CONTENTS

4

FOREWORD

Modern African theology began in 1956 with the publication of *Les Prêtres noirs s'interrogent*. In that volume a group of young African theologians raised questions about how theology was being done in Africa and whether or not things could be different—both theologizing in a more genuinely African way and dealing with topics important to Africans.

Many things have happened in Africa since that first call was made to develop a genuinely African Christian theology. There have been many obstacles to hopes that independence would create a more friendly environment for African cultural values and lead to the development of a theology freed from colonial burdens. Wars, corrupt dictators, and a continuing economic colonialism from the rich North have created an environment where Africans continue to struggle to assert their own dignity and the dignity of their cultures. Even attempts within the Church to convoke an African Synod—a "Synod cooked in an African Pot" as the AMECEA conference called it—meet frustration. Problems of hunger, the flow of refugees, and the explosive urbanization of the continent all point to how much African resources are being strained.

But amid all these signs of worry, hope continues to flow. Evidence is mounting that the evil of apartheid may soon be overthrown in South Africa. The collapse of Marxist regimes in Europe removes one more pillar of legitimacy for dictatorships in Africa. And on the theological front, more and more African voices are being heard, a sign of hope not only for Africa but for the entire world Church.

One of those more hopeful of signs has been the work of Bénézet Bujo. The work of this Zairean moral theologian has been among the most original to appear in Africa. He has published widely on issues of fundamental moral theology and on specific moral issues, especially as they have an impact on Africa. This volume presents his work in a broader, more comprehensive fashion. Blending together concern for traditional African values within the horizon of contemporary social issues in Africa, this book represents the synthetic quality of his theological project. Neither a traditionalist trying to preserve African rural culture in a mindless fashion nor a reformist calling for a move away from African roots, he holds in balance the past and the present, the cultural and the social, and the urban and the rural, in order to develop a theology that speaks to Africans and explains Africa to those outside.

Of particular value in this book is his survey of the origins of modern African theology and his panoramic view of the range of themes that come into play in a fully developed theology. Doctrinal themes such as christology, ecclesiology, and eschatology are mapped out, and pastoral issues such as marriage and care for the dying are elaborated in light of African cultural realities and the exigencies of Christian faith. Bujo admits that this book is but an introductory survey of an African theology, but in showing us the major features of such a theology, he gives us a helpful orientation to what is now available and whets our appetites for what is still to come.

Comparatively little of the work of francophone African theologians has made its way into English thus far. Within its brief compass, however, it lets us see what treasures are waiting there.

This book is a useful guide to theology from that part of Africa, a theology that promises to enrich the world Church with its insight, its sensitivity to culture, its spirituality that reflects so clearly the Gospel as it is being heard and lived in the central and western part of that great continent.

Robert J. Schreiter, C.PP.S.

PREFACE

Since the first publication of this book in 1986, Africa has found itself facing even more problems than it did at that time. In world politics, the collapse of the Berlin Wall clearly marked the end of the Marxist-Leninist regimes in Eastern Europe. This radical change which originated in the Western world acted like a stormy wind that shook deeply the whole of sub-Saharan Africa. Dictatorial regimes whose legitimacy had never been questioned were challenged for the first time in decades. The ordinary people, who for so long were deceived, exploited and plunged into economic chaos by selfish and uncaring leaders, now insist on the adoption of multi-party systems and the unconditional restoration of democracy. What model of democracy Africa will adopt still remains to be seen. Will it copy the Western model with its accent on individualism or will it find it suitable to inculturate modern trends into traditional African wisdom which at one time was such a successful forum for communal democracy? In the traditional setting, individuals could not be free unless they first contributed to the freedom of the whole community and vice versa.

The selection of a political path to democracy is of great importance to Africa at the end of this 20th century. In the same way that the dictatorships so common in Africa were a result of Euro-American influences, it is conceivable that the actual democratic tendency may be just a new strategem to impose upon the Black Continent the domination of the West, together with all the political and socioeconomic consequences this would entail.

Another event that has deeply influenced Africa is the liberation of Nelson Mandela, that hero of the anti-apartheid struggle. The freeing of this great leader of the ANC is a definite step towards the abolition of South Africa's racist policies. In addition, a significant move towards the recognition of the dignity of the black race has been initiated. This new attitude is not to be adopted only in South Africa, but must spread to the whole human race which has to confess its guilt for the indignities and sufferings inflicted on the blacks by powers that once believed themselves the sole masters of history. 1992 marks the 500th anniversary of Christopher Columbus's discovery of America. While it is fit to celebrate this event, it would be unforgivable — not to say criminal — to forget the enslavement of Africans this event brought about and the innumerable deaths that resulted. Africa was deprived of a great many of her sons and daughters who would have been an important component of her vital strength. And still worse, the black slaves, forcefully abducted to a strange land, are still even today victims of prejudice, ill-treatment and social discrimination. Through her children in their places of exiles, Africa, Black Africa, still suffers and is unjustly chastised for the curse which a certain kind of Christianity has imposed on Africans because of the colour of their skin. It was right and fitting that Pope John Paul II during his recent trip to Africa — the first he made to Senegal — in February 1992 should visit the island of Goree in order to beg Africa's forgiveness in the name of Christianity and humankind for the crime of the slave-trade.

John Paul II admits it, "The slave-trade is a tragedy of a civilization that called itself Christian. And the deep causes of this human drama, of this tragedy, can be found in all of us, in our human nature, in sin. I have come here to pay homage to all the unknown victims of this crime, whose names and number can never be known."[1]

It is perplexing and astonishing that history has said comparatively so little of this drama in comparison with the crimes perpetrated by the Nazi regime. John Paul I was right to compare the slave-trade to the concentration camps which have so indelibly scarred modern humanity's conscience. This is the reason why the Pope begs Africa's forgiveness when he declares in the speech he made on the island of Goree: "Throughout a whole period of the African continent's history, black men, women and children were wrenched away from their families and their native lands, brought here to this tiny island, and sold as mere goods and chattels.

[1] Translated from *La Croix*, 25 February 1992

8

"These men, women and children were the victims of a shameful trade, and those who encouraged and practised that trade were baptized Christians who did not live up to their faith. How could one forget the soul-searing sufferings inflicted on those deported from the African continent in violation of the most elementary human rights?

"How could one forget the human lives uprooted and destroyed by slavery? In truth, it is right that this sin of human against human, of human against God, should be confessed in all humility."[2]

If we take into account so many abominable crimes committed against Black Africa, it is not surprising that today the African continent and the Africans of the diaspora should raise their voices and claim compensation for the wrongs committed against them both during the course of the slave trade and during the period of colonization.[3] In fact, the catastrophic economic situation that prevails in Africa today cannot easily be isolated from the longlasting oppression which foreign powers once imposed on it. Besides the loss of human potential and without considering the physical and moral sufferings of slavery, the colonial period initiated and ruthlessly carried out a large scale exploitation of Africa's natural resources. Modern economic practices ensure that this domination continues unabated. The transfer of capital towards the North is just one aspect of this unpleasant reality. This fact should be taken into account whenever the Third World's, and particularly Africa's, over-indebtedness is mentioned. Mature reflection will lead us to discover that it is the North that is in debt to Africa.

It may be necessary to reaffirm here that the dignity that the black person has been deprived of must be restored, not only at the economic, but also at the cultural level. The African's material poverty is deeply rooted in anthropological pauperization (E. Mveng); in fact, the African's culture and religion have been utterly ignored by the colonizing powers who used the African as an object of no value for which any substitute could be found. Contrary to what certain African intellectuals affirm, misguided

[2] Translated from *La Croix*, 25 February 1992
[3] Translated from *Journal de Genève*, 29 February 1992

9

as they are by the economic situation of the continent, it does not seem likely that true African liberation is possible without rediscovering deeply rooted traditional cultural values. In order to attain a sound economic status, it is necessary that black Africans be proud of themselves, and the attainment of such a degree of self-esteem depends entirely on their identifying themselves with their own culture. Economic performance and politics require an inculturation that is truly permeated by African thinking and living.

In this task, African churches have an important role to play. The African Synod planned for 1993 should be a unique forum to assess what has been done and what remains to be done. It is a fact that in their search for justice and democracy within their own countries, many Africans have asked church people to chair national conferences. This shows that, as the continent seeks its way towards a brighter future, Christianity cannot be left out of the process. The confidence that Africans place in church people does not necessarily mean that in the actual circumstances those church people are the best qualified to initiate the democratization process. Another consideration cannot be excluded: it is probable that, following the traditional African way of thinking, the political leader will also be expected to be able to provide a link with the invisible and the mystical. It is a well-known fact that our own political leaders have failed to do that. The confidence that the common people demonstrate towards the churches must urge the latter to pursue the process of inculturation which cannot be limited to the religious sphere but must penetrate all the areas of African life. In this connection, it is to be deplored that the document *Lineamenta* for the African Synod was prepared entirely in Rome without paying much attention to the real problems that affect the continent. "It cannot be ignored", remarks G. Alberigo "that the preparation has been made up to now without giving any say to those most directly interested, the Africans. The text of the *Lineamenta* is disappointing and very inadequate in its references to the crucial aspects of the Christian presence on the African continent."[4]

[4] Translated from G. Alberigo, Chance historique ou bureaucratisation?, in: Concilum 239 (1992) 195-204, here 203.

10

Inculturation which is so fundamental does not seem to permeate the other points on the agenda. It would have been of some importance to demonstrate dialectically the movement between social questions and inculturation; of still greater importance, the domain of social communication — among others — cannot be considered in isolation, and this the *Lineamenta* makes clear. In fact, African tradition attaches great importance to the spoken word. It is evident then that the Synod cannot limit the problem of social communication to evangelization in the sense of a direct and exclusive transmission of the Christian message. The study of social communication must be extended to the political field where government leaders do not hesitate to use both radio and television to misuse and abuse the power of the word in order to exploit the very people who put their trust in them. Some episcopal conferences have already added to and even amended the questionnaire of the *Lineamenta* which they considered too general and too superficial. This work must be pursued further in order to adapt the questionnaire more adequately to the true African situation.

In spite of the imperfections in its preparation, the Synod may still become a decisive event for Africa if the churches mobilize all their forces to give it the right direction and discuss the right questions. The bishops should not consider themselves the only ones responsible for the running of this Synod; let them co-opt the services of competent African theologians; let them not forget either the whole of God's people, including the illiterate mothers and fathers who also have the prophetic role of proclaiming their faith and delivering a message to the churches of Africa and the world.

This book which is now being presented for the first time to the English-speaking public has no mandate to discuss further the problems outlined here. Yet the questions it asked a few years ago have lost nothing of their actuality. It is still pertinent today to ask ourselves who Christ is and what impact he has on the African who does not need to change culture in order to be called a child of God.

To establish the reign of Christ in Africa means to start from the most basic elements of black culture in order to revitalize

11

modern life. It is essential, in fact, that the impact of a truly inculturated Christianity should be made plainly manifest to the African who has been and still is prey to injustice, disease and other social evils.

In which way can Jesus Christ be an African among the Africans according to their own religious experience?

This is the question which a truly African theology must solve. Christology thus understood and taken as a starting point will eventually lead towards a truly African ecclesiology where all the traditional charisms will be given their full rights.

This book is not to be considered as a treatise of African Christology and ecclesiology. As hinted in the preface to the German edition, *African Theology in Its Social Context* is more an initiation to African theology in order to suggest a few basic ideas that might later provide matter for deeper reflection. As to the problems of ethics which have been merely listed here, they will be studied again in more detail in a series of questions on their fundamental yet modern aspects in a publication actually in preparation.

I would like to express my sincere gratitude to St Paul Publications-Africa, Nairobi, for preparing the English edition of this book. This publishing house shows great zeal in promoting theology and Christianity in Africa. I am particularly grateful to Sr Teresa Marcazzan without whose help this translation would never have been published. She has spared neither herself nor her health to ensure the success of this work. Another person who deserves very special mention here is Brother James Conlon who has been a real pillar of strength and patience in the difficult task of carefully verifying the references in detail. His devotedness and his calm approach to problems have been a real source of edification to me. To him, my sincere and brotherly gratitude.

My sincere thanks also go to the Maryknoll publishing house, Orbis Books, who has shown great interest in the book and whose co-publication will contribute greatly to its diffusion. I also wish to express my thanks to Professor Robert J. Schreiter (Chicago) and Dr Edmund Arens (Frankfurt) who have tirelessly advocated the publication of this book.

12

Without some impressive work from my collaborators in the Faculty of Moral Theology of Fribourg, this English translation would never have achieved such sterling quality. The person most involved in the task was Andreas Bamert who really put his soul into his work. He even sacrificed his holidays and his nights to verify that the English translation really corresponded to the original text. His polished work might very well be forgotten unless I mention it here. I feel particularly indebted to him and would like to thank him with my whole heart.

I have taken the opportunity of this new edition to extend the bibliography and to make some amendments to the text of the notes particularly with reference to the work of Charles Nyamiti, my colleague at the Catholic Higher Institute of Eastern Africa

The success of the German edition of this book encouraged me to authorize an English version to be produced. I will be satisfied that this publication has attained its objectives if it helps to stimulate reflection on what a Christianity truly and deeply rooted in African living and thinking should be.

2 March 1992

INTRODUCTION

We can perceive two tendencies within African theology today.

The first tendency dwells exclusively on the African cultural heritage. It is of course true that this heritage must be one aspect of a genuinely African theology, and that any attempt to incarnate the Christian message in African culture must take it into account. However, while this tendency speaks of understanding the faith, of "intellectus fidei", it ignores the contemporary African context. One must therefore ask whether such a theology can speak seriously of either understanding the faith or of incarnating the message of Christ today. Gradually, but firmly, voices are being raised against the advocates of a theology of "inculturation". They are accused of indulging in empty rhetoric and of being disciples of a bourgeois Christianity. It is also objected that this theology is the product of an inferiority complex vis-à-vis the West; it is coloured by an apologetic intent and sustains an aesthetic Christianity. It is not enough to speak of "anthropological poverty" without confronting the post-colonial era which is in many respects responsible for a tragic situation which cannot be remedied by inculturation alone.

Hot on the heels of this group there comes therefore a second, critical group. We must immediately make a distinction between the "Black Theology" of South Africa and "post-colonial Liberation Theology". The difference is not so much one of substance as of the life-situations out of which they emerged. The context is decisive. The South African theology is connected with the "Black Theology" of the United States: it denounces racial discrimination and seeks to establish a Christian way of life which corresponds to the actual context. The great preoccupation of "post-colonial Liberation Theology" on the other hand is the struggle against dictatorship, both domestic and foreign.

In all of this, the problem of culture cannot be ignored. The Black African must rediscover his roots so that the ancestral tradition may enrich post-colonial people and make them adopt a critical attitude towards modern society. Then Africa will be able to breathe with a new life which neither idealizes the past, simply because one is black, nor treats the past as an idol. What is needed is a new synthesis. It is not a question of replacing the God of the Africans but rather of enthroning the God of Jesus Christ, not as the rival of the God of the ancestors, but as identical with God.

It is this second approach which I have chosen to adopt in this work, which I have called "African Theology in Its Social Context". I am convinced that African Theology has a contribution to make to the liberation of all people towards life in its fullness. We would be betraying the Fathers of Africa if we failed to advance their own quest.

The whole tradition of Black Africa treats religion as something essentially liberating. This dimension of liberation persists through all social, political and economic changes.

The subject is treated in two parts. In Part One, I offer an analysis of African society before and during the colonial period. This analysis will enable us to perceive the consequences of the confrontation between the traditional world and the colonial experience. We will then be in a position to turn our attention to the construction of an adequate model for a contemporary African synthesis. This is our task in Part Two.

THE PRELIMINARIES OF AFRICAN THEOLOGY

The present situation of African theology was reached after a series of stages. When we consider the current debate on the subject, we cannot go wrong if we reconstruct the preparatory stages which shaped the actual theology of Africa.

The following exposé starts from the traditional society. This will enable us to elucidate the problems which connect colonialism, and the era of foreign missionaries, with the authenticity of an African Church. In the first place we must discuss how African religion is the very heart of the traditional society, and how colonization and missionary activity together often upset the delicate balance between the basic elements of the old clans and tribes. Only then can we properly understand the reaction of African theologians and authors.

A. THE LIBERATING DIMENSION IN TRADITIONAL AFRICAN SOCIETY

When we speak of the liberating dimension of African religion, we must start from the life-concepts of African clan society. Life is so central that it must be characterized as sacred. This can be shown in three steps.

Long before the arrival of Christianity in Africa, African religion recognized God as the source of all life, especially human life. This will constitute our starting-point in the following considerations (§1). We then proceed to show that while the emphasis is on biological, physical life, the African did not make distinctions but regarded all life as constituting a single, undifferentiated whole (§2). Thirdly, we shall show how both the physical life, and life as an undifferentiated whole, occupied a privileged place in the ancestor-cult (§3). These three considerations will then lead us into a consideration of the basic ethical concepts of traditional Africa (§4).

1. Physical Life as a Dimension of Religious Faith and as Patrimony

It is no longer disputed that the faith in God found in Black Africa was and is for the most part monotheistic. Long before the arrival of any missionaries, most of the tribes of Africa worshipped one God and God alone. The novelty of Christianity for Africans did not consist in its proclamation of one God, but rather in the more complete and definitive proclamation of that one God, whom Africa already knew, and who is also the God of Jesus Christ. It showed more clearly than the African tradition was able to, how this one God wishes to be, and can be in fact, better known and loved.[1]

It is not our task here to examine in detail the monotheistic faith. We are concerned rather to show how closely this faith is connected with the African concept of life. A number of recent studies have shown that God as seen by the people of Africa possesses fullness of life.[2] The Bahema and the Walendu, of Zaïre, say: "Dja lîngî lîngî", by which they mean that God is self-sufficient, in need of no outside support. God is permanent and unchanging: "Dja mbiro î mbi bba." The Banyarwanda and the Barundi call God Imana, and the Bashi Nyamuzinda: both these names signify that God is the source of life and that God acts in a

---

[1] See Th. Kamainda, Deux conceptions monothéistes dans l'Uele, in: *Approche du non-chrétien. Rapports et compte-rendu de la 34e Semaine de Missiologie*, Louvain 1964, 53. Also B. Bujo, Der afrikanische Ahnenkult und die christliche Verkündigung, in: *Zeitschrift für Missions- und Religionswissenschaft* 64 (1980) 293-306, here 298f. V. Mulago, *Un visage africain du christianisme*, Paris 1965. E. Bolaji Idowu, *African Traditional Religion. A Definition*. London 1983, 140-165. J. S. Mbiti, *African Religions and Philosophy*, London 1983. Ph. Pöllitzer, Ancestor Veneration in the Oruuano Movement, in: *Missionalia* 12 (1984) 124-128 etc.

[2] See among others B. Bujo, African Morality: Individual Responsibility and Communitarian Dimension, in: *African Christian Morality at the Age of Inculturation*, Nairobi 1990, 95-102.

living way. God is Creator, God alone can give life, strength and growth.[3] E. Bolaji Idowu tells us that the names for God among the Yoruba and the Igbo, that is, Orise and Chukwu, designate God as the "'Great Immense, Undimensional Source of Beings'",[4] and the Bambuti (pygmies) say that if God were to die, the world would collapse.[5]

All these witnesses testify that God sustains every living thing, but that human beings are the special object of the Lifegiver's attention. God has placed everything at people's disposal: sun, light, rain, good harvests, fertile cattle, health. Even the diviner's medicines owe their power to God, for it is impossible for anyone to be restored to health without God's action.[6] It is therefore not surprising to find for example the Nuba and the Shilluk addressing God as Saviour, Protector and Bestower of the Necessaries of Life.[7] The Sérèer of Senegal pray to God in all difficult situations, especially where there is risk: there are prayers in time of drought, sickness, death, or when the weather is stormy, or a person has bad dreams. They may pray also for social success in situations where the honour of the group is at stake.[8]

What all these prayers express is that God is the source of life, that God not only supports life but rather produces life before people themselves know. So among the Bahema many children are called Byaruhanga (God's property), and among the Banyarwanda Habyar'Imana (God alone begets).[9] The notion of life as a gift of God is very clear too among the Bambuti. "When a Bambuti woman realizes that she is expecting a child, she prepares food and takes a portion of it to the forest where she offers it to God saying: (God) from Whom I have received this child, Take Thou and eat!".[10]

[3] V. Mulago, *Un visage africain*, 121.

[4] E. Bolaji Idowu, *African Traditional Religion*, 160.

[5] P. Schebesta, *Revisiting my Pygmy Hosts*, London 1936, 171.

[6] More details in J.S. Mbiti, *African Religions*, 41- 43.

[7] ibid., 42.

[8] See H. Gravrand, La prière sérèer. Expérience spirituelle et langage religieux, in: *Religions africaines et christianisme*, vol. 1, Kinshasa 1979, 106f.

[9] Similar observations among the Yoruba and Igbo. See E. Bolaji Idowu, *African Traditional Religion*, 160.

[10] J.S. Mbiti, *African Religions*, 42, who quotes P. Schebesta, *My Pygmy and Negro Hosts*, vol. 1, London 1936, 235.

God then is the dispenser of life. But we must not forget another crucial element in Black Africa's concept of life, and that is its hierarchical ordering. Life is a participation in God, but it is always mediated by one standing above the recipient in the hierarchy of being. This hierarchy belongs both to the invisible and to the visible world. In the invisible world, the highest place is occupied by God, the source of life. Then come the founding fathers of clans, who participate most fully in the life of God. Then come the tribal heroes, deceased elders, other dead members of the family, and various invisible beings, including earthly powers, although these belong partly also to the visible world. It seems likely that the cult of tribal heroes is of rather recent origin. Then come beings belonging to the visible world. They include the king, and the queen-mother, as well as those who wield or represent the royal power; the chiefs of clans and the oldest members of families; heads of households; family members.[11]

In short, there is a continuous exchange going on between the visible and the invisible worlds, between the living and the dead. Every member of a clan or family group is obliged to maintain contact with the dead, but is also obliged to keep alive relationships with the living, whom the ancestors have established as their representatives. It will be useful at this point to examine in more detail the hierarchical order referred to above.

In this hierarchical and participatory concept of life, the basic principle is that ancestors live on in their descendants. It is this principle that structures society at its different levels: family, clan, tribe. At the level of the family, the father is the link with the ancestors. At the level of the clan, the mandate of the ancestors is carried by the head of several families together. In the tribe or nation, it is the chief, or king, who represents the ancestors. Kings and chiefs should not be regarded simply as the wielders of secular administrative power. They are connected to the ancestors by a religious bond, they belong to the mystical body of the tribe. Furthermore, it is the function of the chief to give strength and order to his people, although God is recognized as the ultimate

[11] V. Mulago, Eléments fondamentaux de la religion africaine, in: *Religions africaines et christianisme* I, 45-49.

source of life.[12] Placide Tempels grasped this point: "This explains what the Bantu mean when they protest against the nomination of a chief, by government intervention, who is not able, by reason of his vital rank or vital force, to be the link binding dead and living. 'Such a one cannot be chief. It is impossible. Nothing would grow in our soil, our women would bear no children and everything would be struck sterile.' Such considerations and such despair are entirely mysterious and incomprehensible so long as we have not grasped the Bantu conception of existence and their interpretation of the universe."[13] When this conception of life has been understood, it is evident that there is something here which transcends mere biological generation; the function of leaders, at every level of society, is to transmit a life which embraces the whole of human existence, life understood as the totality of the dimensions which constitute the human as a person.

2 . Life as Unity

The conclusion of the foregoing considerations is that life is to be understood in a mystical, or metaphysical, sense. The status of customary rules can be understood only on this basis. Biological life is transmitted by God through the elders and ancestors.[13a] Along with this life, God and the ancestors, and the elders in their respective positions, take care to lay down rules, in the form of laws and taboos, to ensure the prosperity of the society. It is for this reason that such great store is set by the experience of the ancestors, or at least of those ancestors who have lived exemplary lives.[14] Such ancestors had laid down laws, and established customs, which embodied their own experiences, and which they passed on to their descendants as a precious legacy. When the descendants remained faithful to their inheritance, and thus made the experience of the ancestor their own, they remained in living

[12] See B. Bujo, African Morality: Individual Responsibility, 97.

[13] Pl. Tempels, *Bantu Philosophy*, Paris 1959, 63.

[13a] The "elders" are not necessarily the oldest by age. They are the most experienced men and women enriching the community by their wisdom. They can be designated as the "wise ones".

[14] See the various categories of ancestors in V. Mulago, *La religion traditionelle des Bantu et leur vision du monde*, Kinshasa 1973, 41-72.

21

communion both with the ancestor and their own living kin, continually reliving the history of their people and proclaiming the marvels which God had performed for them. Finally, when the living conduct themselves according to the patterns established by the ancestors, they are strengthening the tribe or clan as a whole and contributing to the well-being of each individual member. The forebears protected the tribe and the clan against the forces of disintegration by their careful observance of law and custom. The living must do the same if their society is not to come to ruin.

It is now clear that the living members of this "mystical society" have an inalienable responsibility for protecting and prolonging the life of the community in all its aspects. The details of this responsibility will vary according to a man's status; but father, clan-leader, chief and king, each at his own level, are under a serious obligation to see that the right order established by God and the ancestors is carefully maintained, and each is held accountable for any disorder. One example may suffice. In many tribes, a chief who is no longer contributing to the welfare of his society forfeits his authority, and his subjects have the obligation, for the sake of the ancestors, to remove him from office. In offending against the laws and customs and experiences of the tribe, he is despising the ancestors, and even God, and consequently suffocating the life of his people.[15]

In the African concept of life however it is not simply religious and political leaders who have the obligation to preserve and transmit life. Every member of the community, down to the least significant, shares the responsibility for strengthening the force of the tribe or clan and of each of its members. The morality of an act is determined by its life-giving potential: good acts are those which contribute to the community's vital force, whereas bad acts, however apparently insignificant, are those which tend to diminish life. African society is a real "mystical body", encompassing both dead and living members, in which every member has an obligation to every other.

---

[15] B. Bujo, *African Morality: Individual Responsibility*, 98. Although J.S. Mbiti, *African Religions*, 208, claims that in the African view an offence is never directed to a subject but only towards a superior, he nevertheless agrees that damage is being done to the order of the community, and therefore to its subjects.

22

The head of this mystical body is the founder-ancestor. It is from him that the life-force flows into all the members of the community, to return then to him, not weakened or diminished by its adventures, but greatly strengthened and renewed through the participation of the individual members. A good deed increases the health of the community, and helps to build up the mystical body; an evil deed tends towards the destruction of the community. In the African world-view, all things hang together, all depend on each other and on the whole. This applies particularly to human beings, who are closely connected with each other and with God.[16]

If it is said that the African world-view is anthropocentric, this must not be understood as meaning that there is no place for God within it. The focus of this world-view is life, and life ultimately is God's gift. Even if occasionally there seems to be little consciousness of God and God's position in the scheme of things, when Africans honour the ancestors they are, at least implicitly, also honouring God.

3. The Special Place of the Cult of the Ancestors

It is above all in the ancestor cults of Africa that we see how people envisage life, for it is above all here that they seek an increase of that life-force which flows through the mystical body to which both they and the ancestors belong.

In the Christian tradition, there are fixed times for the worship of God; but the African ancestor-cult is not organized around celebrations of this kind. The individual is not obliged to unite with others in order to honour the ancestors, for they are honoured in every good deed which a person performs in the course of daily life. Africa knows no distinction between individual, social and political life; but life can only be enjoyed in its fullness when the ancestors are remembered and honoured.

---

[16] See e.g. Thomas Aquinas in *Summa contra Gentiles*, III, 122, n. 2948 (Marietti): "Non enim Deus a nobis offenditur nisi ex eo quod contra nostrum bonum agimus".

Communion with the ancestors has both an eschatological and a salvation dimension.[16a] Salvation is the concern of both the living and the dead members of society, for all affect each other and depend upon each other. The dead can only be happy when they live on in the affectionate remembrance of the living; nevertheless, they are stronger than the living, on whom they exercise a decisive influence, since the living cannot hope even to survive unless they render due honour to their dead and continue faithfully along the track laid down by them.[17]

There can be no denying that Africans are above all interested in earthly life, and that they emphasize good fortune and blessing. Yet even in this concern for earthly prosperity, there is an eternal, or eschatological, dimension, for it involves a participation in that other world where the dead live and where is to be found the key to the fate of the living.[18] Further, a person's prospects of ultimate membership in that other world depend on the degree of communion established with it while still living the earthly life.

Funeral rites give expression to the belief that the dead person becomes a guardian spirit who shares life with the earthly family. In some tribes, the deceased may ask "for a little 'fire to warm himself'; he demands a cult."[19] For some days after the death, the late departed may be given a place at meals. The meal especially makes the dead present, and so has a sacramental character. Hans Häselbarth writes: "The deceased takes part in the common meal, at which he is still accepted as a relative: the clan eats with its dead as well as with its living. It is above all the common meal that unites people in Africa, and no one questions the real presence of the deceased, in spite of the separation wrought by death. The holy meal is an effective sign of the communion

---

[16a] Even if we cannot speak of an eschatology in the strict sense of the word, Africans are, in so far as their ancestors and the whole of nature are pointing sacramentally to God, on the way to their salvation, which can be found only in God. From now on we understand the word "eschatology" in this sense, and the same for terms like "protology" or "Mystical Body".

[17] B. Bujo, Der afrikanische Ahnenkult, 294.

[18] See I.P. Laléyé, La personnalité africaine. Pierres d'attente pour une société globale, in: Combats pour un christianisme africain (Mélanges en l'honneur du Professeur V. Mulago), Kinshasa 1981, esp. 141ff.

[19] J. Theuws, Death and Burial in Africa, in: Concilium 32 (1968) 140-143, here 142.

between living and dead. Eating together seals the continuing bond with the dead, while also strengthening the bond between the living. The sacramental dimension of the ritual increases the faith of the participants, in spite of some elements which may seem to the outsider to be very human and even profane."[20]

It is not only in funeral feasts that an inchoate communion between living and dead is experienced. People are conscious of the benign presence of the ancestors whenever they enjoy fullness of life. Good health, numerous progeny, healthy cattle, abundant crops: all these things are felt as signs of the ancestral blessing.

The idea of communion with the dead is central to the world-view of the people of Africa. We may take the funeral rites of the Bahema of Zaïre as illustrating the belief of many African peoples.

Bahema society is patriarchal, and therefore the mourning rites for a deceased father of a family are particularly elaborate. During the funeral rites, the sons, as heirs, all "receive communion" from the hand of their dead father. Grains of millet are placed in the hands of the corpse, and each son licks them off four times, four being the masculine number. The significance is clear: the dead man's children receive his strength, and they must not allow themselves to be unduly depressed by their loss. As their father feeds them with this millet, they ask him not to take food away from them, but to continue to think of them and to strengthen them even in death.

A second rite follows. The sons jump four times over the corpse to receive increase of life and strength.[21]

The idea of survival after death is also expressed in the ceremonies to instal the eldest son[22] as his father's heir. His uncle, the dead father's brother, places his hands on a cow's udder, which he must then begin to milk. Failure to carry out this rite will bring about the death of the cows which the son is inheriting from

[20] H. Häselbarth, *Die Auferstehung der Toten in Afrika. Eine theologische Deutung der Todersriten der Mamabolo in Nordtransvaal*, Gütersloh 1972, 49.

[21] This was suggested to me by R. Ngbape-Kihera-Winyi who kindly gave me his manuscript to read.

[22] Even the youngest son may be recognized as the "elder" son, in case he proves more experienced and judicious than his older brothers.

his father. This would be the greatest imaginable sin against life, for cows are indispensable for survival among the Bahema. The eldest son, moreover, must give to his brothers a share in the cow which he has inherited; ideally each brother receives a calf. The eldest son, having received his father's life-force as well as his possessions, becomes in turn the source of life for his brethren. He must see to it that all the members of the family have everything they need for a decent life, so that they too may become life-givers.

Various other rites practised by the Bahema have the same sense: the father who becomes an ancestor bestows upon his descendants everything needed for a full life: peace, gentleness, fruitfulness, health, steadfastness.

The basic conceptions expressed in the funeral rites of the Bahema are shared by many other peoples of Africa. We might also think of the initiation rites, found all over the continent. They only make sense when we realize that people see life as a gift from God and from the ancestors. Initiation rites are a kind of ordination ceremony in which young people are consecrated especially with their procreative power into the whole community of the living and the dead, but consecrated also to the Creator God and to the ancestors, from whom flow all life and strength.[23]

Hunting ceremonies have the same sense. Before an expedition, God and the ancestors are invoked to ensure a successful outcome; after a good hunt, they are thanked. At sowing and at harvest-time, during famine and drought, prayers are offered to God and the ancestors. Similarly, it would be unthinkable for a marriage-contract to be concluded before the engaged couple had been presented to the ancestors for a blessing.[24] Many other examples could be cited, all making the same point: Life is the greatest gift which God has bestowed upon the people of Africa.

It is not simply God and the exemplary ancestors who are involved in this supreme enterprise of giving and sustaining life.

[23] See M. Ntetem, *Die negro-afrikanische Stammesinitiation. Religionsgeschichtliche Darstellung, theologische Wertung, Möglichkeit der Christianisierung*, Münsterschwarzach 1983.

[24] We suggest the research by V. Mulago, *La religion traditionelle*. id., but with new name Mulago Gwa Cikala Musharhamina, *Traditional African Marriage and Christian Marriage*, Kampala 1985.

Every individual is continually preoccupied with protecting the life of self and family against the malicious attacks of evil spirits, including evil ancestors. These evil spirits can be appeased by special offerings that are connected with diviners, magicians and healers. These specialists are regarded as people who are able to control the forces hidden by God in nature and to use them to help others. These people are not regarded as wholly evil, although there is a dark side to their operations. Admittedly the same forces that help humans can be used to harm them.[25] "Evil spirits" provoke quite different sentiments from those aroused by "good" ancestors, and Africa has developed complicated ritual systems designed to protect life against the menace represented by "the spirits". Wherever one turns in Africa one is confronted with a dominant preoccupation: salvation from all that diminishes life.

The drive towards life is the inspiration of all African religions, often expressed in terms of identity, both individual and group, which must be preserved at all costs. Here we begin to understand the supreme importance of the past for the African: for the secret of life is to be found above all in the hallowed attitudes and practices of the ancestors. In their wisdom is to be found the key to a better and fuller life, and it is therefore crucial that the rites, actions, words and laws which the ancestors have bequeathed to their descendants be scrupulously observed: they are the indispensable instruments of salvation. The way a person treats this inheritance is decisive, for life or for death. The ancestral traditions are gifts of God, they have a truly sacramental character. The life-giving traditions of the past must determine the present and the future since in them alone is salvation to be found.

Something needs to be said at this point about J.S. Mbiti's thesis that the African is exclusively concerned with the present and the past, and has not even the concept of a future.[26]

Mbiti's contention is that the consciousness of the African is restricted to the present (Swahili *sasa*) and the past (Swahili *zamani*). Zamani overlaps with Sasa and the two are not separable. Sasa feeds or disappears into Zamani. But before events become

[25] B. Bujo, African Morality: Individual Responsibility, 98. V. Mulago, *Un visage africain*, 135.

[26] J.S. Mbiti, *African Religions*, 15-28, esp. 22ff.

incorporated into the Zamani, they have to become realized or actualized within the Sasa dimension. When this has taken place, then the events 'move' backwards from the Sasa into the Zamani. So Zamani becomes the period beyond which nothing can go. Zamani is the graveyard of time, the period of termination, the dimension in which everything finds its halting point. It is the final storehouse for all phenomena and events, the ocean of time in which everything becomes absorbed into a reality that is neither after nor before.[27]

According to this theory, the African's conceptual world is solidly tied to the here and now which is perceived as a prolongation of the past. In Mbiti's remarkable expression, it becomes clear that every present experience points backwards to its origin in Zamani. Mbiti says further that "history moves 'backward'". "African peoples have no 'belief in progress', the idea that the development of human activities and achievements move from a low to a higher degree. The people neither plan for the distant future nor 'build castles in the air'. The centre of gravity for human thought and activities is the Zamani period, towards which the Sasa moves. People set their eyes on the Zamani, since for them there is no 'World to Come', such as is found in Judaism and Christianity." It is the past which fascinates them. The 'golden age' lies in the Zamani, and not in the otherwise very short or non-existent future. The "Foundation and Creation myths are of undying interest", for them. There are no myths about the future, no intimations of "the end of the world".[28]

Mbiti's conclusion is that whenever Africans today show an interest in the future, they owe it to Christianity and to Western education. Of course modern developments have altered the old categories: political and social change, and especially the introduction of Western-type education and the experience of political

[27] ibid, 23. The past is designated as "macro-time", whereas Mbiti calls the present "micro-time", ibid., 22.

[28] ibid. 24, note 1. Mbiti says that he knows only of one single tribe, the Sonjo in Tanzania, speaking of an end of the world, suggesting that it might have been caused by the explosion of a volcano in their area. But the thought of it was not of great importance in their lives. - See also idem, L'eschatologie, in K.A. Dickson/ P. Ellingworth eds., Pour une théologie africaine. Rencontre des théologiens africains à Ibadan, Yaoundé 1969, 219- 253. id., New Testament Eschatology in an African Background. A Study of the Encounter between New Testament and African Traditional Concepts, Oxford 1971.

28

independence, have inevitably widened the modern African's vision. The predominance of the old categories is however still perceptible, and explains, among other things, the widespread political instability of the African continent. On the other hand, the phenomenon of independent churches, and particularly of millenarian cults in which people pin all their hopes on a happy life after death, can also be interpreted as reflecting the dislocation of people's traditional time-categories. Once introduced, the concept of future becomes over-valued and exaggerated, and is easily exploited by "Messianic" figures proclaiming the end of the world and future blessedness for the faithful.

Such is Mbiti's theory. What are we to make of it? My own belief is that we cannot hope to reach the heart of the matter until we grant to eschatology its rightful place in the traditional world-view of Africa. We have already seen how important it is for Africans to stick to the rules and customs laid down by the ancestors. Fullness of life is available only to the persons who look to their ancestors for guidance and inspiration.[29] In the varying circumstances of life, the essential thing is to go over again and again the life-story of the ancestors, for therein alone can salvation be found. In spite of the efforts of Max Seckler[30], many theologians are still failing to perceive the essential salvific element in the compulsory repetition of ancient formulas and actions.

The kind of circular thinking, as it may be called, that is characteristic of African culture, meant that people looked to the past for salvation. To some extent, the religious perspective of Africa can be compared to what is nowadays called "narrative theology" which is in fact rooted in the Bible.[31] The ancestral focus may not be always explicitly spelt out, but by repeating traditional rites and formulas people are in fact giving expression to their faith that the ancestors will bring prosperity and ward off ill-fortune. The rituals

[29] I report the results of my research in B. Bujo, Der afrikanische Ahnenkult, 295-297. See id., Die christologischen Grundlagen einer afrikanischen Ethik, in: *Freiburger Zeitschrift für Philosophie und Theologie* 29 (1982), esp. 226ff.

[30] M. Seckler, *Das Heil in der Geschichte. Geschichtstheologisches Denken bei Thomas von Aquin*, München 1964, esp. 29f.

[31] See esp. J.B. Metz, *Faith in history and society. Toward a practical fundamental theology*, New York 1980. See also H. Weinrich, Narrative theology in: *Concilium* 85 (1973) 46-56. In moral theology this concept has been elaborated by D. Mieth, *Glaube und Moral*, Mainz 1976.

are a way of remembering and re-enacting the past, and their repetition constitutes a guarantee of prosperity for future generations. The recalling of the history of the ancestors, with its struggles and its successes, is a kind of "Exodus Theology".

The ancestors are models for the living. Time and history are real, irreversible and unrepeatable. They can be posed the question of the meaning of life. But there is more to it than simply imitating the behaviour of the ancestors. Traditional actions and formulas really bring strength to the living, enabling them to live better in the future.[32] The recalling of the past effects what it signifies. Health, wealth, the enjoyment of life, may be rooted in the past: but it is a past which has meaning for the present and the future. The present is shaped by the past. Indeed, the final consummation, when all things will come to their perfection, is already present in the beginning.[33]

Tradition then, in the African way of thinking, is not to be regarded in a deterministic, much less a fatalistic, way. It is to be regarded rather as a potency, which the individual may choose to actuate or not. Success or failure depends on a personal choice: in freely recalling the life-giving actions and words of the ancestors, a person is choosing life; but in neglecting these things, that person is choosing death.[34] In that sense the individual is responsible for what happens, by deciding whether or not to follow the path which he or she knows leads to life.

The words of Max Seckler are relevant also for Africa: "Time and history are real, irreversible and unrepeatable. They can be posed the question of the meaning of life. History has its categories. Challenge and response; opportunity, cause, motive; duty and its fulfilment; responsibility and blame: people feel that they are part of the march of history and contribute to its ultimate goal. Individual experiences are felt as stages in the pilgrimage which leads to the longed-for consummation."[35]

[32] On the distinction between "model" and "example" see I. and D. Mieth, Vorbild oder Modell? Geschichte und Ueberlegungen zur narrativen Ethik, in: G. Stachel/D. Mieth, *Ethisch handeln lernen*, Zurich 1978, 106-116.

[33] M. Seckler, *Das Heil*, 31.

[34] Similar idea M. Seckler, Heilsgeschichtliches und geschichtstheologisches Denken bei Vergil, in: *Münchener Theologische Zeitschrift* 16 (1965) 111-123.

[35] M. Seckler, Heilsgeschichtliches, 121.

If something like this is in truth the basic stance of the African, then we cannot say, as Mbiti does, that Africans are anchored in some futureless ancient history. Certainly the African cherishes the traditions of the ancestors, but this is so, not for the sake of the past, but uniquely for the sake of the present and future, which it is hoped in this way to render better. The present-day African is thinking eschatologically, of those last times when all will be changed. In looking towards the ancestors, and hence becoming a partaker in their privileges, such an African becomes in turn a source of life for succeeding generations.

Western observers of the African scene, and especially Western Christian observers, have not infrequently asserted that, whatever seeds of truth may be contained in the traditional religions, they generate in their adherents above all a paralyzing fear. God is far away, gone, and the world is under the control of myriads of spirits: this was the vision, say these foreigners, and only Christianity was able to free Africa from its paralysis.

Of course African religion contains negative elements, of course it has a dimension of fear; but so does every other religion. These negative elements should not be exaggerated anywhere. Certainly it is clear that in Africa the good and helpful elements in religion far outweighed the negative elements. As regards liberation, why do so many African Christians return to the traditional practices for comfort in times of crisis? It is by no means unknown for a Christian to seek the sacraments of the Church in the morning and go off into the bush in the evening to consult the witch-doctor. This surely suggests that the African finds more comfort and liberation in the traditional practices than in the rituals of the Christian Church. Thus it may not be asserted too quickly that there is no element of liberation in the traditional religions of Africa.

If African religion is to be classified as a "religion of fear", what shall we say about the Christian message which was brought to Africa, with its devil and hell-fire for all eternity? Did such preaching contribute to the liberation of the people of Africa?

Christian theology has always tended to split humans into body and soul, and to preach the salvation of the soul. Africa could never accept this mutilation of the human being. People in Africa

31

experienced themselves as a unity, living in a network of living relationships with God and with nature. Much of what has been written about Africa's "absent God" must be considered mistaken. God is not far from the African world. All relationships, between person and person, living and dead, and between persons and nature, are rooted in God and point towards God and towards the end of all things in God. They have a sacramental nature, proclaiming that every person's future lies with God. It must also be added that, for the African, God cannot be imagined without God's creation, nor without God's saving will for humankind.

The conclusion must be that Africa has a vision of the future which is not radically different from that of the Judaeo- Christian tradition. We turn now to consider briefly the ethical consequences of this philosophy.

4. Africa's Ethic as a Reflection of Its Anthropocentric Vision

The foregoing exposition suggests that the traditional religions of Africa have their origins in the mystery of life and death. When Africans live this mystery intensively, they discover themselves, and their position in the total scheme of things.[36] In particular, they discover their relationship with the transcendent God who, by the mediation of the ancestors, bestows meaning upon their lives. In such a religion, focussed on the mystery of life and death, humankind itself is naturally the centre of concern, although God is always present, at least implicitly.

This perspective affects above all Africa's moral philosophy, which may be called anthropocentric.

In the African way of looking at things, it was not God but the human who was responsible for the appearance of sin and evil. The moral order is thus seen as a matter, not of the relation between the human and God, but of the relationships between human beings themselves.[37] In fact, many tribes in Africa are

---

[36] See E. Mveng, Essai d'anthropologie négro-africaine: La personne humaine, in: *Religions africaines et christianisme*, II, Kinshasa 1979, 88.

[37] Here I repeat what I said in B. Bujo, African Morality and Christian Faith, in: *African Christian Morality at the Age of Inculturation*, Nairobi 1990, 39-72, here 49-57.

convinced that a human cannot offend God, and this principle applies also to the consequences of sin. Africans believe that they can neither add anything to God, the Creator, nor take anything away from God, so that moral behaviour and its consequences concern only human beings. It is true that God may punish human wrongdoing; but God only does this for the sake of humankind, who otherwise could bring the established order to ruin.[38] God knows everything, and God knows that we love God: God does not need to be continually assured of our love by prayers and ritual offerings. At the same time, there are tribes who say that God's will cannot be known by human beings because God has never revealed it. So the Balambo of Uele, Zaïre: No one has seen God (Nzambe), and no one knows which way God has gone. The only person who could tell us about God was Leh, the first man; unfortunately he died before he could manage to tell others what was God's will.[39]

1. God is however not completely absent from the moral thinking of the African. It has already been shown that prayers may be directed immediately to God, even when the intention concerns human welfare. Furthermore, the rule found in many tribes requiring that the name of God be included when bestowing personal names is best understood as reflecting a theocentric perspective. The Western custom of family names is foreign to African tribes I know. Names are given to babies according to the chance circumstances prevailing at the time of birth, and in this way they constitute a kind of oral diary or history. They also have a future reference, warning perhaps of the enmity between two tribes, or calling attention to God as the source of life. When all is said and done, however, there remains something mysterious and unsaid about African names: in some way, the name is felt as being the actual person. A name cannot be simply transmitted from father to son, nor can a husband simply give his name to his wife.[40] Names

[38] See the interesting study of E. Mujynya, Le mal et le fondement dernier de la morale chez les bantu interlacustres, in: *Cahiers des Religions Africaines* 3 (1969) 68f. For traditional theology see O.H. Pesch, Schwere Sünde und leichte Sünde, in: A. K. Ruf ed.: *Sünde-Busse-Beichte*. Regensburg 1976, 91-106.

[39] Th. Kamainda, Djigi (Dieu), in: *Les Balambo dans le monde*, Viadana (Congo-Zaire) 1960, 45 referred to by E. Mujynya, *Le mal et le fondement dernier*, 69.

[40] Bujo, *Do we still need the ten commandments?*, Nairobi 1990, 27-28. Id., African Morality: Individual Responsibility, 96.

33

have a sacred character, and to call a person's name without good reason is to dishonour him or her. So Africans find it easy to understand why the Judaeo-Christian law forbids "taking the name of God in vain."

2. Generally speaking, "duty" for the African refers to the mutual obligations of human persons.[41] The duties of children towards parents, and the connected obligations towards the ancestors, constitute a major part of African morality. The good life depends not only on the ancestors, but also on the degree of esteem which a person shows for parents and the clan elders. We can see therefore why an African is so careful to look after the elderly and infirm members of the group. When old people are no longer able to make an active contribution to the life of the group, they are still life-givers in the sense that they have wisdom and experience to hand on to their successors. As in the Old Testament, so in Africa: the welfare of the children, and their enjoyment of family possessions, depend on their obedience to the elders and on their willingness to profit from their experience.

3. The focus of African religion is life. It can therefore be easily understood that killing is among the most serious of crimes. Human life, including the life of a stranger, can be taken only in self-defence or when there is a threat to the common good. Even then an individual would never take the life of a clan-member on his or her own initiative.

The following principle is to be maintained: Since the common good must have precedence over the individual good, an individual who is really a danger for the community, or threatens the clan with loss of life or goods, must be simply removed. It may be that the person concerned is unaware of the danger which he or she represents. So sorcerers, and persons with physical or mental defects, who are quite unconscious of their position, are classed with murderers and thieves and done away with. It is not that death is sought for its own sake, but only that killing is right when it contributes towards the welfare of the clan as a whole. At the same time, the individual is not just the helpless victim of society, for the clan has an obligation to guarantee the

---

[41] See C. Adimou, Vodù et christianisme, in: *Bulletin Secretariatus pro non christianis,* 28/29 (1975), 29-39. E. Mujynya, *Le mal et le fondement dernier.*

development of each of its members. The clan can only prosper when it cares for the individual.

This is not to deny the danger that the individual will be treated as of little account in this system. Too much emphasis on the interests of the clan can obscure individual freedom and individual rights. Christianity has clearly a corrective role to play here.

4. In the field of sexuality too the overriding goal is to provide for the continuance of the clan. For the most part, sexuality is seen in the context of procreation. To separate sexual activity from its procreative function, or to be incapable of performing this function, is to inflict serious damage on the clan, including its dead members. The community of the ancestors is composed not only of dead members of the family, but also of the living descendants, who form with the dead a single "mystical" community. The dead live in the remembrance of the living who conduct with them a continual dialogue. The dead live on too in their descendants, so that numerous progeny can only be welcomed. For many Africans, childlessness and celibacy are crimes against humanity.

Here we run into the problem of trial marriage and polygamy,[42] as well as into the question of priestly celibacy. The ancestor cult so dominates people's thinking in many tribes that life-long celibacy is regarded not only as abnormal but as a serious aberration, an offence against the primitive command "to increase and multiply", and an offence too against "immortality".[43] Nothing like enough thought has been given to this matter in the Roman Catholic Church.

5. Another element in Africa's anthropocentric ethical system concerns the transmission of property. The right to private property is deeply rooted in the traditions of Africa. It is by struggling for a degree of independence, and by winning security for himself and his family, that a man shows his quality, and his fitness for marriage.

The community dimension of possessions must however be stressed. The final aim is never personal enrichment. Property

---

[42] For more depth see later chapter on Marriage spirituality in Africa, and B. Bujo, Die pastoral-ethische Beurteilung der Polygamie in Afrika, in: *Freiburger Zeitschrift für Philosophie und Theologie* 31 (1984) 177-189. See also J.S. Mbiti, *African Religions*, 26.

[43] ibid., loc.cit.

belongs to the individual, but only so that, in case of need, it may be placed at the disposal of the community. Attached to all property is the notion of stewardship and ministry. Africa is of course changing under the impact of foreign cultures, but in traditional times no one questioned the obligation of clan-members to help each other, and no one was allowed to go without the necessaries of life. Conversely, any kind of laziness or parasitism was vigorously denounced. As for theft, this was never tolerated. Thieves might find themselves barred from marriage, and might even be punished by mutilation. Theft was of course an offence against the owner of the stolen goods, but it was also, and above all, an offence against the whole clan.

The attitude to property was not the same in traditional Africa as it is in modern Christian thinking, and attitudes to theft were therefore likewise different. It is not always easy to answer the question, "Who, in African thought, is the real owner of this piece of property?" Several tribes in what are now Zaïre, Rwanda, Burundi and Uganda regarded the king, or "Mwami", as the ultimate owner of everything in the kingdom, people included, and no one would think of accusing him of theft whatever he did with his subjects' property.[44] Within the context of the power allowed to him by the ancestors, he could do what he liked with everybody and everything. One cannot deny that this concept of monarchical government is outdated in the modern world. Many harmful consequences arise from the abuse of this concept by contemporary dictators in Africa.

6. Traditional Africa had strict rules about speech. Lying was an abomination, especially when it damaged the clan. Of course this meant that there was a danger that people would lie when this could further the interests of the clan. Such an act indeed was not regarded as lying at all, but rather as clever and virtuous, a sign that one loved one's clan. Otherwise however lying was regarded as morally wrong and harmful. So if a person had embarked on some project which involved him or her in falsehood of some kind, he or she had to abandon it, for it could only lead to disaster. Similarly, negative and destructive criticism of a neighbour's plans were to be avoided, since they could bring ruin both to the

[44] See E. Mujynya, *Le mal et le fondement*, 73f.

36

plans and to the neighbour. Explicit curses were even more vigorously condemned, for curses could effect what they expressed.

7. We may ask finally whether Africa recognized a morality of pure thought, or whether it considered only external acts as having a moral character. The matter has often been discussed. Some observers have maintained that African morality took no account of thoughts, regarding them as neither good nor bad.[45] Such a contention cannot however be reconciled with the many African proverbs which attach blame or praise to secret thoughts as well as to secret actions. We may ask furthermore, if Africans attributed a moral character only to external activity, why did they make the *heart* the seat of moral behaviour?[46] Also the fact that merely coveting another man's wife or possessions was regarded as sinful, since it was an attack on the life of the clan as well as on the life of the individual, shows clearly that Africans were also concerned with the morality of thoughts. African tradition makes it plain that people considered that thoughts and intentions, as well as external acts, had a moral character, and deserved to be considered "good" or "bad".

It is the task and indeed the duty of Christianity to judge the religion and the morality of Africa and rectify them where necessary. We may however now proceed to ask whether, in pursuing this task, the Christian Church has in fact really corrected the African tradition or whether it has not rather too often sought to obliterate it.

B. THE COLONIAL PERIOD AND FOREIGN MISSIONARIES

Europeans did not find a paradise when they arrived in Africa. They did however find functioning societies in which people lived reasonably prosperous and happy lives. We must now ask whether Europeans in Africa have really made an effort to understand and

---

[45] ibid., 77. For additional bibliography see F. Mitima, La place de l'intention dans l'acte moral chez les Bantu. Thesis for the Licentiate, Kinshasa 1980.

[46] See on this B. Bujo, African Morality: Individual Responsibility, 100-101.

preserve the religion of Africa, or whether they have not been more concerned with furthering European political and economic interests than with helping the people of Africa.

A quotation from the Murundi priest Michel Kayoya deserves pondering:

The consciousness of the colonized

In 1885 at Berlin our Continent was partitioned. Without consulting anyone they had pity on our misery.
They came to save us from earthly misery
They came to educate us
They came to civilize us
This 'Act', known as the Berlin Act, has humiliated me for a long time.

Every time I come across its date, I feel the same contempt still.
That a man despises you
So be it
One thinks of it for a day
Then it is finished
That a people despises you
You
Your father
Your mother
Your People
That is the last straw
The last straw of indignation that a human heart can 'stomach'.

The worst it is that they taught me this date. They made us memorize it. For a whole lesson they named all the participants in this Berlin Act.
Their exceptional qualities
Their diplomacy
The motives which urged the one and the other.

Before our impassive faces they displayed the results obtained:
The pacification of Africa
The Benefits of Civilization in Africa
The courage of the explorers
Disinterested philanthropy

38

And no one
Absolutely no one pointed out this injury
This shame which followed us everywhere
That a man!
An equal!
Should meddle in your affairs without consulting you at all
It is flagrant lack of courtesy which any well-bred heart resents.[47]

There are many Africans who would find themselves in agreement with Michel Kayoya. And even if his criticism is directed in the first place against the colonial governments, the Church can by no means wholly escape censure. For the missionaries worked hand in glove with the colonial power. They did indeed preach the gospel. But they preached it within the framework of a tainted system.[48]

5. The Colonisers

Most of the Europeans who came to Africa at the beginning of the colonial period did not do so with the idea of helping or "civilizing" the black people, but for reasons of self-interest. The plundering of the Congo by the Belgians is well known, and the story need not be repeated here. The Europeans regarded themselves from the outset as superior to the unarmed Africans whom they now met for the first time. The blacks were of course the vast majority, but socially, politically and economically they were treated as a minority. Hegel's judgement on the Blacks as unruly and "savage" is well known.[49] The general attitude of the whites was that there was nothing in Africa which really deserved the name of "human". As Balandier has noted, the Africans were just

[47] M. Kayoya, *My father's footprints*, Nairobi 1973, 75-76. For the situation before 1885, and esp. the slave trade, see B. Adoukonou, *Jalons pour une théologie africaine*, I, Paris/Namur 1980, 35-55.
[48] B. Bujo, What kind of Theology does Africa Need? Inculturation Alone is not enough, in: *African Christian Morality at the Age of Inculturation*, Nairobi 1990, 119-130, here 120.
[49] G.W.F. Hegel, *The Philosophy of History*, New York 1956, 218- 222.

cheap labour, tools which the colonisers could use to become rich.[50]

Various means were used by the colonizers to subdue the Africans which can be grouped under three headings: the drawing of frontiers, the manipulation of traditional chiefs, the attitude to traditional religion.

1. The Drawing of Frontiers

Right across Africa frontiers were drawn without any reference to the ethnic distribution of the people, or to customary law. The people were simply ignored. From one day to the next, tribes and clans and even families found themselves split by new boundaries. The Europeans had issued their decree, and henceforth people must beg permission if they wanted to cross frontiers to visit their relatives. The Churches followed the same procedure: dioceses and vicariates were set up for the most part without any reference to tribal sensitivities.

In a similar spirit of total disregard for the people of Africa and their history, Europeans proceeded to give names to geographical features like mountains and rivers, and to invent names for new "nations". An African joke illustrates the situation. In Eastern Zaire there is a river called "Aruwimi" which received its name in the following way. It comes from "Alubi nini?": the Lingala way of saying, "What is he talking about?" Once upon a time, a European explorer, coming to a river, said to one of his African companions, "What is the name of this river?" The African, not understanding the European's accent, turned to one of his fellows, and asked, "What is this man saying?" The European took this as an answer to his question, and so jotted down in his notebook, "River Aruwimi", which was his version of "Alubi nini?" The name "Cameroon" has a somewhat similar origin. It comes from the Portuguese word "cameroes". The Portuguese found so many crabs in the River Wuri that they talked of "the river of crabs". Eventually that become "camerones" in Spanish, "Cameroon" in

---

[50] See G. Balandier, *The Sociology of Black Africa (Social Dynamics in Central Africa)*, New York 1970, 21-56 esp. 23.

40

English, "Cameroun" in French and "Kamerun" in German, and the inhabitants were turned into some version of "Cameroonians".[51]

2. Traditional Chiefs

Under the colonial régimes, the old chiefs of Africa lost their independence, and were required to act simply as the agents of their new masters and to advance their interests. They were puppets. If they objected to this role, they were sacked. Blukwa, the Chief of the Bahema, was an example. The colonialists found him uncomfortable because he was not prepared to be a simple yesman, and he was therefore sent into exile. The contempt for traditional authority, and its virtual destruction by the colonialists, produced alienation in African society.

3. Traditional Religion

Colonial governments waged vigorous campaigns against polygamy, the cult of the ancestors, so-called sorcery and witchcraft, and the like. In these campaigns the missionaries acted as powerful allies of the secular authority. This writer would not wish to maintain that the missionaries were wholly wrong in this field. Corrections to the tradition were needed. But the damage done to the balance of the traditional societies by the wholesale condemnation of the whole religious and social structure was often disastrous.[52] The ancestor-cult, for example, was central to the religious and social structure, and to destroy it undermined the whole fabric of society. There will be more to say on this subject when we come to sketch an "African theology" in Part Two of this study.

As far as art is concerned, artistic treasures are of course to be found all over Africa. The African people however know nothing of "art for art's sake". For them, art is bound up with the whole of life, and especially with religion. Ola Balogun writes: "For the African, art is something altogether wider and deeper than the

[51] See L.J. Calvet, *Linguistique et colonialisme*, Paris 1974.
[52] See G. Balandier, *The Sociology of Black Africa*, 348-55 and passim.

typical collector of folklore might imagine..."[53] It is "a sign, a proof even, of the real presence of the supernatural."[54] W.A. Umezinwa says similarly that the African uses art to express his sense of the mystical.[55] Art is a way of narrating the experience of life and death, an expression of the history of the clan, in this world and the next. Art shows us African spirituality with its inarticulate aspirations, sharpening the belief that lifeless things too have souls.[56]

The Europeans had different criteria for judging art, and they exhibited the world "to the colonized people from the standpoint of the artists and intellectuals of the Western ruling classes."[57] So African works of art, which had profound meaning for the world of the African, were often not estimated at their real value. Sometimes these objects, especially masks and carvings — provided of course that they satisfied European standards — were carried off to the colonial motherland. Modern Africans who want to study the art and history of their own country have great difficulty in gaining access to the ancient masterpieces of their people. As soon as an African *objet d'art* landed up in an American or European museum, it ceased to belong to Africa. The foreign museum treats it as its own property, and makes full use of the law to prevent the African country where it originated from claiming it back. A good example of this was reported by Israel Katoke. There is in the British Museum a mask from Benin which is of great cultural and religious significance. It should clearly be returned to Benin, but "the English say that a decision of Parliament is necessary before this can be done. But no Parliamentary decision was required when it was stolen. In cases such as this we must find a solution which is based on equity and mutual respect."[58] The situation is the same with respect to important

[53] Ola Balogun, Form and expression of African Arts, in: *UNESCO Courier* 5/1977.

[54] ibid.

[55] W.A. Umezinwa, The Idiom of Plastic Figures in Chinua Achebe's Novels, in: *Religions Africaines*, vol. 2, 125- 133. See also the text of Ben Enwonwu, in: *Panafricanism Reconsidered*, Berkeley 1962, 349-352.

[56] Ben Enwonwu, op. cit., 351.

[57] Ngugi wa Thiong'o, Literature and Society, in: *Teaching of African Literature,* Kenya Literature Bureau, Nairobi 1968.

[58] Interview with Israel Katoke in *Sunday News* (Tanzania) of 23/4/1978. [As quoted by A. Imfeld, *Verlernen,* 59, and retranslated into English.]

documents which are irreplaceable as sources for the study of African history. Anyone who wants to write a thesis today on colonial or mission history must somehow find the money and time to tour numerous libraries in Europe and in the U.S.A.; and even then he or she may not find it easy to obtain access to the relevant documents.

All this may suffice to show how Africa has been robbed of its culture and, so to say, rendered bloodless. A crucial part of its life-force has been taken away from it. The colonial powers were not content merely with replacing the African social system with another. They had recourse to every available means to impress upon the black people, in word and deed, that they were inferior to whites and, furthermore, that the inferiority was due to the colour of their skin.[59] Black people had to be convinced that their inferiority was irreversible, unchangeable. For it was clear that if black people were not kept down in this way, that would be the end of colonialism. If black people began to rethink their position and to see themselves as the equal of white people, the consequences would be incalculable. There would be no more peace, and colonies would cease. These rules must therefore be strictly observed; they alone could guarantee the survival of the colonies.[60]

6. Foreign Missionaries

It has already been noted that missionaries and governments worked hand in hand in Africa. Governments sometimes refused to admit missionaries who were not of the same nationality as the colonial power. One example may suffice for many. The Flemish Scheut Missionaries were actively supported by the Belgian King in their evangelizing work in the Congo. The underlying idea, among others, was that these missionaries, belonging to the same

[59] See L. Kesteloot, *Négritude et situation coloniale*, Clé, Yaoundé 1970, 35f: "You have to convince the people with a coloured skin that they start believing that the inferiority of their situation is the result of their difference in skin pigmentation": Directive of a Ministry, according to Kesteloot.

[60] ibid., 87, note 45. "From the moment that the black man starts to regard himself as the equal of the white, the consequences can not be foreseen". For more texts see in: O. Bimwenyi-Kweshi, *Discours théologique négro-africain*, Paris 1981, 87ff.

43

nation as the colonizers, would be more likely than foreigners to support the policy of the government.

It can at least no longer be seriously disputed that foreign missionaries were encouraged to co-operate with the colonial governments. A Belgian handbook for colonial administrators for instance insisted that the work of civilization was not in the hands of the government alone, but also in the hands of missionaries, for religious teaching and religious institutions were of great importance. The colonial endeavour had three arms: government, mission, commerce, and all had to work together. Government officials had a keen sense of their obligations towards missionaries, and were punctilious, for example, in visiting mission schools.[61]

The co-operation of church and state extended also to the strictly religious field. The attacks on polygamy and the ancestor-cults of Africa were conducted by both secular and religious authorities. In Zaïre, church and state were very severe on ancestor-cults. A document issued in September 1923, in Stanleyville, now Kisangani, by the Superiors of the Belgian Congo Mission lists customs considered harmful to public order, and requested the colonial government to take action against them. The customs included: offerings to spirits and ancestors; co-operation in ancestor rituals; dancing and hunting ceremonies; magical or religious rites on the occasion of a birth, or the appearance of the child's teeth, or circumcision, or a girl's puberty, or marriage, or illness. Likewise forbidden were traditional rites in honour of the ancestors performed before a hunting or fishing expedition, and carvings representing the spirits of the dead.[62]

The measures against African rituals and customs were executed by the colonial government with the full co-operation of the missionaries of the Catholic Church. These were deeply marked with the Roman spirit, which took it for granted that the

[61] See Receuil à l'usage des fonctionnaires et des agents du service territorial au Congo belge (Directives for government agents in the Belgian Congo), Bruxelles 1930, 57f, as quoted by O. Bimwenyi-Kweshi, ibid., 88f:"... Government agents, whatever their personal opinions, are under strict obligation to help the Christian missionaries... especially in the regular frequentation of the mission schools by their pupils".

[62] See G.E.J-B. Brausch, Le paternalisme, doctrine belge de politique indigène (1908-1933), in: *Revue de l'Institut de Sociologie* 2 (1957) 215.

catechism used in the Roman West was entirely suitable for Africa, and considered that in the work of evangelization the emphasis must be on stamping out savage and immoral customs. It is hardly an exaggeration to say that the missionaries adopted an attitude of blanket condemnation of African culture in all its aspects. African converts were required to turn their backs on the whole of their tradition and the whole of their culture. Only then was it considered that the Christian faith had truly taken root in their souls.[63] The Ghanaian, Alex Quaison-Sackey writes: "Perhaps worse was the deliberate attempt to eradicate or destroy our cultural heritage. Since drumming, for example, was considered by the church to be a heathen practice, African Christians were at once cut off from the wellsprings of their culture — the rhythms of African music and dance. ... African medicine, too, was regarded as inferior; and if you were an African Christian, you were expected to seek help from the doctor at the hospital, not from the African herbalist, who had come to be styled the 'witch doctor' or 'medicine man'. And yet it was the herbalist who throughout the ages had cured our fevers and our diseases. His knowledge of local herbs could have been used in the development of curative medicine in Africa, but instead he was condemned, and no distinction was made between him and the trickster or 'juju-man', who preyed on our superstitious beliefs."[64] As for the names bestowed in baptism, it never occurred to the missionaries that they could give to their African converts names taken from their own African tradition. African names were unworthy of Christian faith. In the long run, African Christians themselves came to adopt the same mentality and rejected their traditional names as pagan. Lawino complains in Okot p'Bitek's *Song of Lawino*:

> "My husband rejects Acoli names,
> Meaningful names,
> Names that I can pronounce.
> He says
> These are *Jok* names

---

[63] Ngugi wa Thiong'o, Church, Culture and Politics, in: *Homecoming: essays on African and Caribbean literature, culture and politics*, London 1972.

[64] A. Quaison-Sackey, The African Personality, in: *Africa Unbound*, London 1963, 38-58, here 52-3.

And he has nothing
to do with *Jok*.

He says
He has left behind
All sinful things
And all superstitions and fears.
He says
He has no wish
To be associated any more
With the devil.

Pagan names, he says,
Belong to sinners
Who will burn
In everlasting fires:
Ocol insists
He must be called
By his Christian name!"[65]

Alex Quaison-Sackey similarly shows how in the nineteenth century Ghanaian names were deliberately anglicized to show that their bearers were Christian and "civilized". His own name, "Sekyi", was turned into "Sackey" by his great-uncle, a nineteenth-century Methodist minister, and his maternal grandfather took the name "Quaison", "Son of Kwei", to show his learning while he was still a schoolboy in 1896.[66]

When one bears in mind what was said above about the significance of names for the African sense of individuality and personhood, one can understand what this cultural and religious oppression meant to the people of Africa.

One might multiply examples of the general insensitivity of European missionaries towards the people of Africa and their culture. The Roman breviary, divided into the four seasons of spring, summer, autumn and winter, was simply placed ready-made into the hands of the African clergy, for whom such seasons had no

---

[65] Okot p'Bitek, *Song of Lawino*, New York 1969, 127-8 [or combined with *Song of Ocol*, Nairobi 1972, 124]

[66] A. Quaison-Sackey, op.cit., 52.

46

meaning. Africans learned Christmas carols full of references to snow and frost. The Holy Eucharist is still celebrated with bread and wine, although the ordinary African Christians have no idea what wine is and cannot imagine how it can bring them into a closer relationship with Christ. It is not thus that one prays with Christ, and we are wrong to claim his authority for such regulations. Can we really think that the God who became man would refuse to accept the Black Africans with their *ugali*, corn-meal mush, or *fufu*, manioc-meal mush, or palm-wine? Would the Guest on the road to Emmaus refuse our invitation and insist on going further, in spite of the lateness of the hour, simply because we had prepared for him only *ugali* or palm-wine? [67]

And what are we to say of the ban on polygamy? Basing themselves on the theology dominant in the nineteenth century, the missionaries taught that monogamy was the only permissible form of marriage. Even the Second Vatican Council put polygamy on the same level as so-called "free love".[68] Pope John Paul II insisted that polygamy directly contravened God's plan and was an offence against women's equality with men.[69] Apart from the fact that such statements ignore the whole pedagogy of the Old Testament and of Christian history, it must also be said that the Christian Church and the earlier missionaries failed to understand the African institution of marriage. It is not within the scope of our present concern to pursue this matter fully, but a few general points may be recalled.[70]

One of the principal reasons for polygamy was the failure of a first marriage to produce children. The fulness of life, received from the ancestors, was seen in one's posterity. To die childless was to be consigned to oblivion, cut off from the earthly community, for only one's own children could render one proper honour. For that reason, children are always a blessing. If the first wife cannot bear children, the husband, with her agreement, will take a second. Polygamy thus cannot be separated from religion; it

---

[67] B. Bujo, What Kind of Theology?, 121.
[68] *Gaudium et Spes* 47.
[69] *Familiaris Consortio* 19.
[70] In more detail in B. Bujo, Die pastoral-ethische Beurteilung, 177-189.

is rooted in the African "protological-eschatological" faith.[71] There was also a socio-economic dimension to polygamy: it promoted the survival of the clan by making each family self-sufficient. Children provided the peasant family with its indispensable labour force, and polygamy was the best way of ensuring abundance of children. It should also be noted that polygamy contributed to the stability of marriage by rendering divorce superfluous, and providing for the maintenance of all women: there was hardly prostitution in traditional Africa. Polygamy further created vast and intricate relationships between families and thus multiplied friendships and promoted peace within the clan.

It is not being maintained that all polygamists were motivated by these high considerations. Nevertheless, the institution of polygamy needs to be taken seriously. It cannot be right to brutalize human beings in the name of some so-called Christian law, nor to present catechumens with an undignified choice between "baptism or wives" which seems to have precious little to do with the love of Christ.

These few examples may suffice to show how inadequate was the understanding of Christian missionaries of the basic structure of African society. Many vital elements were destroyed, and the opportunity of really incarnating the Christian message in Africa was lost. It is not denied that there were in the African cultural tradition elements which had to be challenged by the Christian gospel. The failure was to distinguish between the positive and negative elements in the culture.

I am not underestimating the pioneer work of some missionaries in the area of culture. Who could forget the Franciscan, Placide Tempels, whose careful research provided modern African theology with its first inspiration? [72]

Then there was Siegfried Hertlein, who produced important studies on the misionary activity of German Benedictines in southern Tanzania, who were open very early on to the idea of an

---

[71] In patrilineal tribes the eschatological expectation is bound to male offspring. On this more in B. Bujo, Die pastoral-ethische Beurteilung, 180

[72] Esp. Pl. Tempels, *Bantu Philosophy.* Id., Catéchèse bantoue, in: *Le Bulletin des Missions* 22 (1948) 258-279. Id., *Notre rencontre*, Léopoldville 1962.

African theology.[73] Men like these however were exceptions, and they had little effect on the attitudes of the early missionaries as a body.

Some remarks should be made especially about the work of Siegfried Hertlein. He writes with a strong bias in favour of the early missionaries. No doubt we should have understanding for these missionaries and be generous in excusing them. Hertlein's work however is written simply from the standpoint of the missionaries and colonizers, and shows little understanding of the point of view of the powerless people they evangelized and governed. In many ways his work reminds us of the criticisms offered by Michel Kayoya which were quoted at the beginning of this section. He speaks at length about the works of compassion for which the missionaries were responsible, about the courage of the missionaries and about their solid Christian education which was confronted with the rough life-style of the Africans (pp. 25-32). He has however nothing to say about the sensitivities of the Africans or about how they reacted to all these good things which were poured out upon them. He never considers the possibility that the Africans may in their hearts have experienced the whole missionary endeavour as an offence, and as destructive of their way of life.

Contemporary African theology arose out of the feeling of black people that they had not been taken sufficiently seriously by white people, including missionaries. African theology is a reaction. Its various forms may now be considered.

C. THE POSITION OF AFRICAN AUTHORS AND THEOLOGIANS

From all that has been said, one point emerges with clarity: to attack the African religious system is to condemn all those human beings who live by it, and to deprive them, not only of their

---

[73] See S. Hertlein, *Wege christlicher Verkündigung. Eine pastoral-geschichtliche Untersuchung aus dem Bereich der kath. Kirche Tanzanias.* Erster Teil: Christl. Verkündigung im Dienste der Grundlegung der Kirche (1860-1920), Münsterschwarzach 1976.

natural dynamism, but of their very identity. From the African point of view, this is the worst of all sins.

Africans were "brainwashed" by the colonial system. Some of them nevertheless were able to perceive the danger which threatened their continent, and they sought to bring this to expression in writing. The most prominent of these writers have been not theologians but secular authors, and they challenge not only the colonial system, but also the missionaries, whom they accuse of failing to appreciate the values of African culture. It was only later that theologians found the courage to tread the path first traced out by their non-religious compatriots.

I have tried to take this development into account in what follows. We speak first of those early prophetic voices who wanted to rehabilitate the values of African culture and who prepared the way for the later independence movements. In the light of this pioneering work, it will be easier to understand the demands of theologians for a Christianity adapted to the African world.

7. The Consciousness of African Authors

All began with the movement known as "Negritude". It was foreshadowed at the end of the nineteenth century with the Negro slaves in the USA and in the "Pan-Negro" ideas of people such as W.E.B. Dubois (1897), but the real founding fathers of Negritude were three Africans studying at the Sorbonne in Paris in the 1930's: Léopold Sédar Senghor, Aimé Césaire and Léon Contran Damas. The movement had its origin in the experience of racial discrimination which, while it was less brutal in France than in the United States, was still effective enough to arouse the resentment of the African students in Paris. They put aside their countries of origin to see themselves simply as "Negroes", and they began to write.[74] Negritude is a kind of act of faith in Africa, in its past and in its destiny. The three pioneers wanted to think and write as Africans, believing that only in this way could they recover their identity and their freedom.[75] Senghor put it thus in later years:

[74] See R. Mercier/M. and S. Battestini eds., *L.S. Senghor, poète sénégalais* (Littérature africaine, 3), Paris 1964, 9.

[75] ibid., loc.cit.

50

"Our renaissance will be more the work of African writers and artists than of politicians. We have seen from experience that there can be no political liberation without cultural liberation."[76] He found the proof of his thesis in the United States of America, where white people were more prepared to listen to the demands of black people after writers and artists from the black community had restored to their people their dignity and showed their true face.[77] In the same way, if Africans want to win recognition in the world as a whole, then they must gain respect for their sculpture, their music, their dance, their literature, their philosophy.[78] According to Frantz Fanon, "the concept of negritude ... was the emotional if not the logical antithesis of that insult which the white man flung at humanity."[79] For Aimé Césaire, colonialism robbed Africans of their humanity. The colonialists soothed their conscience by looking at the African as a kind of wild animal, who could only understand brutal treatment.[80] Africans could only react in one way: by glorifying themselves and their culture. This was the only escape from the colonialist trap. "The unconditional affirmation of African culture has succeeded the unconditional affirmation of European culture."[81]

Frantz Fanon wrote: "The native intellectual who takes up arms to defend his nation's legitimacy and who wants to bring proofs to bear out that legitimacy, who is willing to strip himself naked to study the history of his body, is obliged to dissect the heart of his people."[82]

On doing this, the intellectual discovers "that there was nothing to be ashamed of in the past, but rather dignity, solemnity and even glory."[83] When Senghor was asked if he did not think that negritude was only a kind of racism in reverse, he vigorously

[76] L.S Senghor, No Political Liberation without Cultural beration (trans. from: L'esprit de la civilisation ou les lois de la culture négro-africaine), in: *Senghor: Prose and Poetry*, London 1965, 71.

[77] ibid., loc.cit.

[78] ibid., loc.cit.

[79] F. Fanon, *The Wretched of the Earth*, New York 1968, 212.

[80] Aimé Césaire, *Discourse on colonialism*, New York 1972. Also F. Fanon, op. cit., 210ff.

[81] F. Fanon, *The Wretched*, 212-3.

[82] ibid., 211.

[83] ibid., 210.

denied that he wanted to shut up the people of Africa in some isolated cultural ghetto. On the contrary, he said, he wanted to open them up to the "universal" in dialogue with men and women from all corners of the human family.[84]

At the same time, there can be no denying that the whole negritude enterprise did involve redefining black people vis-à- vis white people. We can understand why black people felt the need to speak out loudly and clearly, and especially why they gloried in, and thanked God for, those features which were mocked by white men: the shape of the head and nose, the thick lips.[85]

Some African authors were principally interested in exposing how their culture had been destroyed by the colonial government. Others were more concerned to criticise the methods of the missionaries. We have already spoken of Alex Quaison- Sackey and Okot p'Bitek. We must also mention Mongo Beti and his book *The Poor Christ of Bomba* which appeared in Paris in 1956. The Bomba of the book is a mission-station in the Cameroon, founded and still directed by Father S. Drumont. The Christianity preached there is an imported Christianity which preceded colonialism and has simply no point of contact with African traditions. While the Father relies on an external Christianity, and believes in radical conversion, he fails to perceive that the Africans have not really understood the Christian message at all. We see this from the missionary's cook, who explains to the priest that the first Christians of Bomba were only interested in the new religion because they wanted to learn the key to white people's secrets. They believed that in this religion they would find the secret knowledge which enabled white people to produce aeroplanes and railways and all the other marvels of modern technology. The Africans wanted to know how it all worked. But instead of opening up these important secrets, the missionaries had begun by talking about God and souls and eternal life, which were matters already familiar to the Africans.[86] The same point is made by the young

[84] See Senghor's reply to the Italians 1962, in: R. Mercier/M. and S. Battestini eds., *L.S. Senghor*, 10.

[85] See the poem of Bernard Dadié, Je vous remercie mon Dieu, in: R. Mercier/M. and S. Battestini eds., *Bernard Dadié, écrivain ivorien* (Littérature africaine, 7), Paris 1964, 38f.

[86] See the presentation of *The Poor Christ of Bomba* in: id. eds., *Mongo Beti, écrivain camerounais* (Littérature africaine, 5), Paris 1964, 19.

administrator, Vidal, when he says that Drumont is an artist whose function it is to mould people as if they were pieces of pottery and to determine what shape they shall have.[87] As long as Father Drumont remained at the mission station, he believed that he was offering the Africans a Christianity which they could understand. It was only when he went deep into the bush that his eyes were opened and he realized that Christianity had not at all displaced the traditional religious faith of the people. At best, there was an uneasy co-existence between the two faiths. The missionary at first retained the hope that the gospel would in the end prove a real leaven in Bomba to transform the whole. This hope was shattered when he perceived that even among his "chosen few", the traditional "immoral" customs retained all their power. Suddenly he realized that baptism had not changed the Africans in the slightest, and that Sunday Mass likewise had failed to convert the inner man. Discouraged, Father Drumont packed his bags and returned to Europe for good.[88]

Mongo Beti successfully showed how an imported Christianity which took no account of the African religious tradition was bound to be seen as nothing more than an element of the colonial system. It is not so much a question of blaming the missionaries, who certainly did a great deal of good, as of exposing a mentality which did a great deal of harm. In his own way, this author too can be regarded as one of the architects of negritude.

Today the idea of negritude is regarded as superseded. It was invented to defend the black man against the colonizer, but it never managed to get beyond the stage of an antithesis against colonialism's thesis. In the post-colonial period, we are dealing with a new thesis, neo-colonialism, and to this, it is objected, the disciples of negritude have no antithesis to offer. All they can do is repeat their old antithesis which has no relevance for the new situation.[89] In truth, negritude was originally conceived, not so much for the sake of the Africans, as for the white public to whom it was primarily addressed. Some of its critics would say that it was essentially a product of capitalism, for it equated Africans

---

[87] ibid., 29.

[88] cf. ibid. 19-21.

[89] D. Kambembo, La négritude en question, in: *Synthèses* 1 (1969) 117f.

with the exploited proletariat. It is therefore incapable of dealing with the new dialectic of the consumer society.[90] Today geographical colonialism is no more. What we have to deal with now is neo-colonialism, a situation in which the heroes of negritude have not seldom themselves turned into the new oppressors. The colonialists have been routed, and the "freedom-fighters" can now take over their privileges. So it has come about that the major preoccupation of the modern advocates of negritude is how best to fill their own pockets. Political independence has turned into a kind of collector's item, beautiful to contemplate, but quite useless as far as ordinary people are concerned. This development was strikingly illustrated by Aimé Césaire in his play "Une Saison au Congo". The play is about four expatriate bankers in the Belgian Congo in the 1950's. Three of them panic when independence for the Congo is announced. The fourth remains calm and reassures his colleagues. He has been in Africa for twenty years and claims to know all about "the savages". The only things they understand are physical pain on the one hand and flattery on the other. What then do the savage Africans want today? It is clear that in the new "independent" situation the Africans will be looking for rich pickings: they will want to be presidents and members of the parliament, senators and ministers; and they will want credit notes and bank accounts and cars and villas and luxurious living. The basic principle now must be to overfeed the savages, to stuff them full with all the things their greed demands. Then they will become meek and humble of heart, simple to manage. Since we are talking about the representatives of the people, it is they who will persuade the population at large to accede to the proposals of the bankers. So there will be a fruitful conspiracy.

When the fourth banker has finished his speech, the other three give him three cheers and cry, "Long live Independence!"[91]

Seen in this light, negritude can be a danger, for it tends to bring to power persons who are even worse colonialists than the white persons they have displaced. Another solution is however

[90] ibid., 118f.
[91] See A. Césaire, *Une Saison au Congo*, Paris 1966, 21. quoted by D. Kambembo, op.cit., 123.

54

possible, and we can here listen to Joseph Ki-Zerbo. He offers three basic guidelines. "First, what are the main features of the social organization and conception of the traditional African society? Next, what are the principal elements of the present crisis? And finally, what prospects and what transcendent structure will emerge to create the new African society for her to obtain a higher sociological level?"[92] Ki-Zerbo suggests that the new African society start from the traditional conception of authority, in which the ancestors are included. He insists, in opposition to what is often said, that the traditional African concept was not of some absolute, dictatorial authority, and believes that contemporary African leaders should look more closely at their own traditions. In the traditional African society, furthermore, there was an egalitarian spirit which meant that there was no exploited class, and great store was set by hospitality. There was also a spirit of tolerance: religious wars were unknown.[93] All these elements could be used to construct a new society which would combine African tradition with elements from modern Western society. Their tolerant and virtually classless tradition should help modern Africans to avoid the class struggle which has been a characteristic of Western society: equality and fraternity should come naturally to Africans. Ki-Zerbo offers this summary of his ideas: "To conclude, I would say that negritude has been sufficiently sung and celebrated in story; it is time for a transformation — not for a new or so called new, culture, consisting of a cloudy veneer over merchandise coming from the West or from the socialist countries. This new culture must stem from an African basis; it must resemble the great African trees, whose heads are thrust up into the civilization of the Universal but whose roots, on the other hand, plunge deeply into African soil."[94]

There is then no dream of recreating a "Paradise Lost" in modern Africa.[95] Africans want to bring the world of their ancestors to new life in their world, for only thus can they find true life for themselves and for their children. Theologians too have

---

[92] J. Ki-Zerbo, African Personality and the New African Society, in: *Pan-Africanism Reconsidered*, Berkeley 1962, 267-282, here 268.

[93] ibid., 268-271.

[94] ibid., 281-2.

[95] See B. Bujo, What Kind of Theology?, 122.

recognized the necessity of bringing African culture into the categories of Christianity. Nevertheless the question remains whether these theologians have really gone further than the negritude movement.

8. The Reaction of the Theologians

We can distinguish three phases in the movement towards an African theology. Firstly, we speak of the investigations of Placide Tempels. Secondly, there is the African consciousness to consider. Thirdly, we shall consider criticisms offered by the modern generation.

1. Placide Tempels and his Inspiration.

The real starting-point of African theology came from a European Franciscan missionary in the Belgian Congo, Placide Tempels. His great effort was to try and understand the African cultural heritage so as to be able the better to announce to the people of Africa the Good News of Jesus Christ. His classical study, "La Philosophie bantoue" (Elizabethville, 1945), analyzed the fundamental elements of the African cultural tradition in order to get at the thought-categories and the religion of the people of Africa. One of his most important findings was that the focus of the whole African religion and world-view generally was vital force, or "life-force". Tempels went so far as to claim that for the African "to be" was the same as "to have life-force". Only when we have grasped this, he thought, can we begin to understand African philosophy and religion, and thus also the actions and behaviour of Africans.

Tempels' object in all this research was to devise a system of catechizing, and a pastoral programme, which would fit Africans.[96] Before he wrote his book, he had undergone a "conversion" to the African people. He himself distinguished three

[96] See Pl. Tempels, *Catéchèse bantoue.* Id., *La christianisation des philosophies païennes,* Anvers 1949. Id., *Notre rencontre,* 2 vols., Limete-Léopoldville 1962. Additional bibliographical data in A.J. Smet, La Jamaa dans l'oeuvre du Père Pl. Tempels, in: *Religions africaines et christianisme,* vol. 1, Kinshasa 1979, 265-269.

stages in his personal pilgrimage. In the first stage, he tended to see himself as a kind of omnipotent and omniscient shepherd, demanding from his flock respectful obedience. The second stage was the phase of adjustment, in which he sought to make the Gospel intelligible by clothing it in terms drawn from the language and experience of the people. Finally there ensued a real exchange between pastor and people, leading to a dialogue between the cultures concerned.[97]

Tempels realized that the African quest for life, for fertility (fatherhood and motherhood) in its most comprehensive form, the yearning for communion with other beings, was not an aspiration confined to the Black Continent. We were dealing here with a fundamental human instinct, common also to Europeans. It went deep into human nature itself, and the uncovering of an African philosophy could therefore help white people too to discover themselves.[98]

Tempels linked up the African search for life with the Johannine Gospel in which Jesus said that he had come to bring life and to bring it in abundance (Jn 10:10). If Jesus is truly the Way, the Truth and the Life, then he is the final answer to the aspirations of the whole human race and not only of Africans. All human cultures manifest the human longing for fullness of life. In seeking to christianize these cultures, missionaries must put aside their own Western culture, repudiate it even, in order to adapt themselves to their people of adoption. This is the price they must pay in order to win the people to whom they are sent. This is how the living Christ encounters the many races and cultures of people, it is thus that Christianity is born, and thus that different people come together to uncover the gospel in common. The missionary's focus must be the Living Christ, who knows no barriers either of time or of cultures.[99]

One of the fruits of Fr Tempels's researches into African culture was the Jamaa Movement which he founded. Unlike Nyerere's similarly-named Ujamaa, it was exclusively pastoral in

---

[97] See Pl. Tempels, Le Père Placide Tempels s'explique, in: *La voix de Saint Antoine* 6 (1967) 7. Reference in A.J. Smet, *La Jamaa*, 259.

[98] See Pl. Tempels, *Notre rencontre*, I, 38.

[99] A.J. Smet, *La Jamaa*, 258.

orientation. Tempels himself indeed refused to treat Jamaa as a movement at all, but saw it simply as Christian discipleship;[100] "Jamaa" is the Swahili word for "family", and Tempels tended to use it as a comprehensive term for the Christian life.

When we consider how the word came to be used however in the life of the Catholic Church in Zaïre, we cannot deny that it denoted, more narrowly, a particular group which gathered round Fr Tempels in the 1950's. Whatever Tempels may have wished, "Jamaa" became a proper noun, denoting a specific movement in the Church.[101]

"Jamaa" has in fact much the same sense as the old word "ecclesia". It means an assembly of the people. Tempels said that Jamaa is a vital religious experience of the Church as a living community of priests and people.[102] It is neither a sect nor a confraternity nor a new movement, but nothing more nor less than the Church itself. He insisted that he was only continuing the traditional teaching of the Church in simpler language and in a way which corresponded to the culture and sensitivity of the people to whom he was ministering.[103] He believed that in this way Africans could be introduced to a Christianity which was no longer alien but truly of their own "flesh and blood".[104]

Tempels can rightly be called "the Father of African Theology". No doubt, he often speaks of "adaptation" where we might today prefer "incarnation". But he began the process, he laid the foundations on which Africans were able later to build.

2. The Birth of African Theology

The first African who can be called an African theologian was Vincent Mulago, a Catholic priest from the then Belgian Congo who graduated from the Urban University in Rome in 1955. He wrote a thesis entitled, Life Unity among the Bashi, Banyarwanda and Barundi, part of which was published in 1956 with the title, L'Union Vitale Bantu, ou le Principe de Cohésion de la

[100] Pl. Tempels, Notre rencontre, I, 27.

[101] In regard to the origin of Jamaa, see A.J. Smet, La Jamaa, 259.

[102] Pl. Tempels, Notre rencontre, I, 11 and 29.

[103] ibid., 84.

[104] Pl. Tempels, Le Père Pl. Tempels s'explique, 8.

58

Communauté chez les Bashi, les Banyarwanda et les Barundi (Annali Lateranensi XX (1956), pp.61-263). Also in 1956, a Rwandese priest, Alexis Kagame, attracted attention with his La Philosophie Bantu-Rwandaise (Brussels, 1956), while a group of African priests published Des Prêtres Noirs s'interrogent (Paris, 1956).

All these works contributed to the development of reflection on a genuinely African theology. For the most part however they amounted to no more than preparatory steps towards this goal. They spoke, for example, about the blood-pact as an opening towards the Eucharist, and about African solidarity as a parallel to the Mystical Body. There was also an attempt to use traditional African symbolic behaviour as the basis for an African sacramental theology. The first African theologians used terms like "adaptation", "Africanization", and "indigenization", which gave the impression that all that was required was a kind of *aggiornamento*. No one spoke yet of "inculturation" or "incarnation". Nevertheless, with all their limitations, these early African theologians laid foundations which were to be of great importance for the future of Christianity in Africa.

As early as 1960, there was a passionate discussion about African Christianity and African theology among the academic staff of the Faculty of Catholic Theology in the University of Lovanium in Kinshasa. At a seminar held on 29th January, a debate took place between Alfred Vanneste, the Dean, and Tharcisse Tshibangu, then a student, later auxiliary bishop of Kinshasa. A report of the proceedings was published in the *Revue du Clergé Africain*.[105] The term "African theology" was still so new that people only dared to use it in inverted commas.[106]

Tshibangu called his talk, *Vers une théologie de couleur africaine?* (Towards a theology with an African slant).[107] He maintained that Africa must have an African Church.

[105] Débat sur la "théologie africaine" in: *Revue du Clergé Africain* 15 (1960) 333-352.

[106] As far as I can see, Vanneste had spoken of an "African Theology" already in 1958. See his contribution: Une Faculté de Théologie en Afrique, in: *Revue du Clergé Africain* 13 (1958) 233-235. History of this concept in H. Rücker, *Afrikanische Theologie, Darstellung und Dialog*. Innsbruck/Wien 1985.

[107] Th. Tshibangu, Vers une théologie de couleur africaine?, *Revue du Clergé Africain* 15 (1960) 333-346.

Africanization was not simply a matter of personnel, of having African bishops and lay leaders; nor was it enough to adapt the liturgy, and to reform parish and pastoral structures. Thought must be given to an "African theology".[108] African studies and African theology must go hand in hand.

Tshibangu proposes certain elements which could serve as guiding principles for an African theology. He mentions life-force, symbolism and intuition as key factors in Africa's vision of reality. Religion however had the pre-eminence, and it was here, Tshibangu believed, that missiologists must find those latent "seeds" which would prepare pagans for the gospel. The religious life of the African contained many elements which could be considered as "latent theological seeds". If these "seeds" could be purified, they could be used as "religious analogues" to illuminate theological problems. At least, they could serve as the foundations of purified African religious categories capable of theological formulation.[109] In his student days, Tshibangu was hesitant about speaking too definitely. Later on, he committed himself a little further in saying that a theology with an African "slant" seemed to be possible. Once African culture was seen as having its own system and thought-structure, there could be developed an African theology with its own special "emphasis".[110] Vanneste responded to Tshibangu's position in a well-known paper entitled, *D'abord une Vraie Théologie*, (First, a True Theology).[111] Since Christianity was a "universal religion", it must have a theology which would be valid for all cultures and races.[112] More than any other science, theology must take very seriously its vocation to pursue truth.[113] Down the ages, theology had made use of a variety of philosophical systems, such as Platonism and scholasticism. This however was to be regarded as a kind of necessary evil. Very often the originators of Christian philosophical-theological systems were unaware that they were borrowing from

[108] ibid., 333f

[109] ibid., 341.

[110] ibid., 344.

[111] A. Vanneste, D'abord une vraie théologie, *Revue du Clergé Africain* 15 (1960) 346-352.

[112] ibid., 346.

[113] ibid., 347.

60

elsewhere. The most recent theological authors had aimed at a strict "universality", and even modern philosophy, with its acceptance of the relativity of knowledge, strove for universal truth.[114]

There is a distinction to be drawn, Vanneste maintained, between theology and the demands of the pastoral ministry. The latter concerned catechesis, and was the province of the missionary. The thinker and writer would of course insist that the African context be taken into account when the gospel was preached. But it was not the function of theology to lay down the route which adaptation had to take. Theology operated at a higher level, at the level of the whole church, and method in theology resembled method in the sciences, where apparently useless and quite disinterested research had resulted in almost miraculous technical progress.[115]

As for African theology, Vanneste could not see that it was useful to try and use primitive concepts which were frankly magical in inspiration.[116] Adaptation should mean rising to a higher level, not descending to a lower.[117] Vanneste wondered whether it was really possible for Western-educated Africans to revert to primitive conceptions which they had in fact outgrown. Furthermore, society was evolving, and it was more than likely that the African culture of the future would be more like the culture of Europe than that of ancient Africa. Vanneste had difficulty in accepting the thesis that the African culture of the future would be radically different from the culture of Europe.

Vanneste concluded that theology in Africa had to be part of the worldwide theological endeavour. African theologians had nothing to gain from shutting themselves up in a world of their own. They could only end up by being regarded as second-class theologians, if that.[118] In the ensuing debate, however, most theologians took the side of Tshibangu.

In 1968, the Theological Faculty of Kinshasa organized a further colloquium on African Theology. Vanneste spoke rather more

[114] ibid., 347f.
[115] ibid., 348.
[116] ibid., 349.
[117] ibid., loc.cit.
[118] ibid., 351.

delicately, but without shifting his basic position. Hardly any of the other speakers took his side.[119]

We might at this point be permitted to offer a judgment on the Tshibangu-Vanneste controversy. Without entering into all the details of the discussion, it seems fair to say that Vanneste's general position was authoritarian and unduly simplified the history of theology. Theological pluralism is after all perceptible even in the New Testament itself. There is a difference between patristic and scholastic theology, and there are also different strands within each of these traditions. There is a difference between the theology of the East and that of the West. Christianity has not grown up in a kind of culture-free vacuum but has always been in living dialogue with the surrounding culture. A good example of the relation between theology and culture is the problem of the titles given to Christ, of which more will be said later.

I would like to ask here if we can regard Heribert Rücker as correct in presenting Vanneste as the saviour, the prophet even, of African culture.[120] He writes: "Vanneste's theory of an 'African theology' has not found it easy to gain a hearing, although, far from seeking to make African culture obey some universal law, he emphasizes the importance of the personal search for truth" (p.55). Rücker classifies Tshibangu's theory as "Platonic" and thinks that his "theology from above" owes much to popular Platonism. Vanneste, on the other hand, he sees as representing rather the earlier school of Parmenides (p.51). He considers further that Tshibangu and other advocates of the possibility of an African theology treat revelation as a set of ideal, timeless principles contained in the Bible and in the tradition of the Church. So-called "supra-historical" propositions may assume a variety of forms, but they can always be recognized by their claim to absolute validity. They are beyond the scope of all verification, or even of comprehension, and are incapable of further development. These "absolute" propositions are the unchangeable basis for any further Catholic theological statements, they constitute the framework of truth within which all theology must take place. (ibid.)

[119] See the collection: *Renouveau de l'Eglise et nouvelles églises*, Mayidi 1969.
[120] H. Rücker, *Afrikanische Theologie*, 55.

Certainly a theology of adaptation may be criticised, but one may not go too far. There are statements in Tshibangu's work which imply something more than a mere theology of adaptation.[121] In his *Le Propos d'une Théologie Africaine*, published in 1974 when the author was already a bishop, he maintains that the Bible should be transmitted from the Holy Land directly to Africa, without being first "treated" by Europe (p.37). Conventional Western biblical scholarship must be looked at critically, so that the Africans can receive the Bible, not as filtered through Western culture, but with their own eyes. It is true that Tshibangu thought that the magisterium of the Church should exercise control over the development of an "African" theology (p.6); but we are not obliged to see in this stance Rücker's "Platonism", which would place revelation beyond all temporal, spatial or cultural contexts. The very fact that Tshibangu appeals to the magisterium as arbitrator shows that he takes theological research seriously and does not regard it as simply a matter of "adaptation". The whole of biblical revelation and Church tradition is to be subjected to unbiassed scrutiny. His concern for his official function is here to be understood as a call for dialogue between theologians and the Magisterium.

These observations do not absolve Tshibangu from the charge of adaptation, but they do bring into question the validity of Rücker's exaggerated criticisms. Even if we accept the justice of his criticisms of Tshibangu and of others who follow the same line, I cannot agree with his interpretation of Vanneste. Rücker rightly says that Vanneste "speaks only of theology's abiding effort to arrive at a better understanding of truth" (p.54, n.43); he is proposing a universal theological effort and not a "universal theology" as opposed to an "African theology" (p.53 and p.54, n.43). We must however consider the context of Vanneste's defence of his thesis of the "search for truth". If we read carefully what Vanneste and Tshibangu have to say, we can see that the latter does not speak only of adaptation but also of certain elements which must find their place in the elaboration of an African theology: intuition (cf. *Vers une Théologie*, pp.339-340), human fulfilment

---

[121] Th. Tshibangu, Vers une théologie, 344. The pronouncements of revelation need to be reflected on the traditional African background.

(ib., p.341), life-force (ib., pp. 338-339) and symbol (p.340), which last-named Rücker so strongly emphasises.[122] If we now turn to Vanneste's text, we may wonder whether he accepts these elements as valid instruments in the search for truth. Some of his statements suggest that he does not. He says that he does not feel obliged to take into account in his theology many so-called African "concepts" (p.349). When he speaks of sacramental theology, he says only that it must take into account the findings of modern psychology and philosophy. He clearly means only Western psychology and philosophy, for he dismisses many African concepts as primitive and magical and useless for theology (pp.349-350). Moreover, Vanneste believes that it is only within the Western concept of personhood that a valid and genuinely liberating theology of original sin is possible. The implication is that African ideas of solidarity and social thinking cannot be fitted into any theory of original sin. Indeed, for Vanneste, it would be a backward step to take such elements as starting-points for theology (p.350-1).

Vanneste sees all within the context of European culture, whose achievements have been so impressive. European culture was able to achieve such a high level of development, he maintains, because people had the courage, and the humility, to allow themselves to be taught by Greece and Rome (p.351). In clear terms, Africans have not yet started to query their "undeveloped" culture. It is high time that they agreed to be guided by the developed, and proven, culture of Europe. Only then will they be able to advance to a higher theological level. Hence the insistent appeal: Let us first have a true theology!

All this Rücker seems not sufficiently to have considered. What, for example, does it mean to speak of "a true theology"? It is clear from what has been said that Vanneste's objections are not merely directed against a "theology of adaptation". Rather he thinks that the European method of searching for truth is the only possible method, and that it should therefore be adopted also by

---

[122] If H. Rücker, *Afrikanische Theologie*, 90, is quoting Vanneste in regard to "symbol", it is understood that such thoughts are of a later phase in the Belgian theologian. From personal experience at the Catholic faculty of Kinshasa I know how he gradually refined and revised his earlier positions, something which cannot be found by the study of his writings only.

Africans. Does not this mean that his "truth" is some abstract, metaphysical reality, independent of all subjective or cultural context? Yet truth can reach Africans only through the vehicle of a time- and place-conditioned culture. When they ask questions about truth, they cannot abandon their African humanity, as indeed Vanneste in one place fully recognizes (pp.347-8). But must this mean, as Vanneste contends, that the African is outside the universal theological effort towards the truth, and is therefore condemned to remaining permanently a second-class theologian?

This can hardly be so, for Tshibangu, himself an African theologian, is at pains to stress the importance of rational criticism if African theology is to contribute to humankind's universal striving towards the truth (e.g., pp.344-5).

Vanneste's sharp distinction between "pastoral" and "theology" is also significant for his understanding of "truth". Such a distinction is typical of a metaphysic separated from any subjective or situational context, and of a type of Western mentality which, for example, similarly separates body and soul. Within this perspective, theology is concerned with "truth-in-itself" and ignores the meaning of truth for actual people and real situations. This approach however fails to recognize that truth can only be discovered and conceptualized within the context of life.

It is not irrelevant to recall these complex problems at a time when many theologians feel challenged to ask whether there is not a real sense in which "praxis" must always precede "theory".

The statements of Vanneste and Rücker are then open to serious objections. One would not however wish to deny that Tshibangu is following in the footsteps of the advocates of negritude and never gets beyond speaking about the possibility of a genuinely African theology. One could understand this tentative approach in a student, but why was it that after he became a bishop Tshibangu never got beyond this stage of posing the question? For even now he is still speaking about the "possibility" of an African theology.[123] It seems that Tshibangu became an official administrator so soon after completing his studies in Louvain

[123] See Th. Tshibangu, The Task of African Theologians, in: K. Appiah-Kubi/S. Torres, eds., *African Theology en Route*, Maryknoll 1977, 73-79. Id., *La théologie comme science au XXe siècle*, Kinshasa 1980.

that he was unable to pursue further theological research. He was totally taken up with an endless round of journeys, meetings, congresses, continually being asked to give lectures and to write forewords for books. Thomas Kramm calls him a theologian "manqué" whose output was restricted to giving conferences.[124] Tshibangu never got to the point of criticising the presuppositions of theology. He is not the only African theologian who has never moved beyond the theology of the negritude movement. Even today, when we read the works of a number of African theologians we get the impression that their real aim is to show the world how religious Africans really are, and how the basic elements of their traditional religion can be used as the "raw material" for the construction of an African theology. But no effort is made to work up this "raw material" into a genuine, even if tentative, theological synthesis. Even the work of O. Bimwenyi-Kweshi is not yet a genuinely African Christian theology, but only a preparatory ethnological analysis.[125]

Voices are being raised today demanding a rethinking of this conventional approach to African theology. People are demanding a theology which can really lead to an incarnated Christianity in Africa, according to the wishes of the Bishops of Africa and Madagascar expressed in the Rome Synod of 1974. [126]

3.Towards a Renewed African Theology

The criticism of a renewed African theology is twofold. One criticism concerns the lack of any theological synthesis, which we have just been speaking of. The second complaint is that many, if not most, African theologians do not proceed contextually. They ignore the actual, post-colonial situation, and, instead of trying to construct a new liberation theology for Africa today, remain stuck in the position of the outdated negritude movement.

[124] See Th. Kramm, Ein Afrikaner zwischen Staat und Kirche, in: H. Waldenfels ed., *Theologen der Dritten Welt*, München 1982, 82-95. See the review of O. Noggler in: ZMR 68 (1984) 304.

[125] See O. Bimwenyi-Kweshi, Discours théologique négro-africain, Paris 1981. See also the review by L. Clerici in *Neue Zeitschrift für Missionswissenschaft* 1983. The same perspective in: B. Adoukonou, *Jalons pour une théologie africaine*.

[126] This is the purpose of the periodical *Select*, published by L. Mupagasi OP in Kinshasa.

These criticisms may be considered under two headings: Theology and African Tradition, and Inculturation and Liberation Theology.

(a) Theology and African Tradition

There are a number of African theologians who have tried to go beyond the initial question of the possibility of an African theology. Charles Nyamiti and John Mbiti are perhaps the best known, but there are others, like J.S. Pobee,[127] E.J. Penoukou[128] and M. Ntetem.[129]

Mbiti's special effort was to try and compare African concepts with the biblical message.[130] The effort was admirable, but it cannot be said that the attempt to incarnate Christianity in the African context was a success. The material he collects however is interesting, and the parallels he draws between the biblical and African world views are important for further theological research.

Charles Nyamiti is more ambitious than Mbiti. He tries to re-state in systematic fashion the Catholic dogmatic tradition in terms of African tradition, drawing on ethnological material. Unlike V. Mulago, Nyamiti goes beyond simple anthropology into genuine theological research. He calls on other African theologians too to transcend a mere preliminary clearing of the ground and at long last to proceed to tackle the propositions of theology itself.[131]

The criticism that can be made of Nyamiti is that he wants to fashion his African theology on the model of the European

---

[127] J.S. Pobee, *Toward an African Theology*, Nashville 1979.

[128] E.J. Penoukou, Réalité africaine et salut en Jésus-Christ, in: *Spiritus* 89 (1982) 374-392.

[129] M. Ntetem, *Die negro-afrikanische Stammesinitiation.*

[130] See e.g. J.S. Mbiti, *New Testament Eschatology in an African Background*, London 1971; id., Some African Concepts of Christology, in: G. Vicedom ed., *Christ and the Younger Churches*, London 1972, 51-62.

[131] See e.g. C. Nyamiti, *African Theology. Its Nature, Problems and Methods*, Pastoral Papers 19, Kampala 1971, Id., *The Scope of African Theology*, Pastoral Papers 30, Kampala 1973. Id., *African Tradition and the Christian God*, (Spearhead 49) Eldoret (Kenya) 1977. Of special value is id., *Christ as Our Ancestor. Christology from an African Perspective*, Gweru (Zimbabwe) 1984.

speculative tradition.[132] Indeed he takes the propositions of European scholastic and neo-scholastic thought as his starting-point.[133] It is impossible to avoid the impression that Nyamiti simply wants to rebuild the scholastic or neo-scholastic, edifice, but using African rather than scholastic or neo-scholastic terminologies.

Nyamiti shows initiative. But anyone thinking about his method would wonder whether many of the problems discussed in Western theology are relevant to African Christians. What the Church needs to do today is to uncover the vital elements of African culture which are stamped on the African soul. Once the African heritage has been clearly understood, then it can be placed alongside the biblical and patristic traditions, and progress will be possible. Our guide in the construction of an African theology must be, apart from African tradition, the Bible and the Fathers of the Church. They must be the light which will show up the limitations and the inadequacies of any theological system, however brilliant.[134]

Anyone who wants to construct an African theology must take the basic elements of the African tradition and interpret them in the light of the Bible and the Fathers. At the same time, however, it has to be recognized that in the post-colonial era many Africans no longer know their traditions. Many of the old African values are simply disappearing. Traditional hospitality is nowadays being abused as a pretext for parasitism. In traditional Africa, no one was allowed to become a burden to anyone else. After three days, guests were expected to help their host in the fields and in general to earn their keep.

Polygamy represents another way in which traditional customs can decay. No doubt, polygamy has to be criticised. It is however quite wrong to regard it as a kind of prostitution. In polygamous unions, each woman could lead a satisfying life, with her dignity recognized. Today this tradition has been stood on its head. The

---

[132] See also H. Rücker, Charles Nyamiti, in: H. Waldenfels ed., *Theologen der Dritten Welt*, 54-70.

[133] A telling example is his latest book *Christ as Our Ancestor*.

[134] On this see B. Bujo, La théologie africaine, quelle direction et quelle méthode? in: *Select* 17 (1984) 135-139. This procedure does not imply a non-critical reading of biblical and magisterial text, as H. Rücker insinuates.

first wife is no longer consulted before the husband takes a second. Indeed she may well be left to cope with life's problems on her own, a state of affairs which could never come about in the traditional situation. There again the second wife is no more willing than the first to share her husband's love with a rival.

As for sexuality, this was valued in traditional Africa, not as a source of pleasure, but for the sake of descendants. The ancestors laid upon every man the responsibility to provide survivors both for himself and for his clan; he had therefore an obligation to sire as many children as possible. When we have understood this, we can understand to some extent the mentality of certain politicians who have children all over the place without having the slightest intention of ever marrying their mothers, although the ancestral tradition would have prescribed marriage.

The independent churches and sects of modern Africa reveal elements from the old tradition, such as belief in the power of the spoken word, or the role of women. The latter is especially remarkable in the Kimbanguist Church. Somewhat similarly, Christians of good standing have been known to have recourse to diviners and sorcerers in times of crisis.[135]

Examples might be multiplied of how the ancient traditions of Africa have been perverted in the contemporary situation. In spite of all the modern perversions, however, we must attend carefully to the traditions of the past since these traditions, consciously or unconsciously, still have a great influence on people's mental attitudes. The crisis of contemporary Africa can be solved only by those who have understood its historical roots and can see them in the light of the actual situation. Only thus can a new society arise which is both truly African and truly modern.

The Christian Church has an important part to play in helping this new society arise. The future of Christianity in Africa depends on getting the right balance between the old and the new. All Christian preaching must help to restore the confidence of the people of Africa in their cultural heritage. Let there be an end to the situation in which students and professors are endlessly

---

[135] For a systematic treatment of this topic see Buakasa-Tulu-Kia-Mpansu, L'impacte de la religion africaine sur l'Afrique d'aujourd'hui: Latence et patience, in: *Religions africaines et Christianisme* 20-32.

presenting learned papers about African theology, while no one thinks about helping the ordinary Christian in the countryside. What Africa needs today is an enlightened catechesis which knows how to distinguish between traditions which are still alive in the hearts of men and women, even if only implicitly, and those which have truly died. This catechesis needs to be able to discriminate so that it may be seen which traditions should be maintained, or perhaps recalled from a kind of cultural limbo into which they may have fallen.

This task does not belong to theology alone; other disciplines must also be recruited. Depth psychology, cultural anthropology, popular art, sociology, all have their indispensable contribution to make. When the material has been gathered, then it is the task of theology to sift it and see how it can be used to proclaim the word of God. Everything that is available must be pressed into service to promote a real understanding of the Reign of God in which Africans can be truly themselves. Catechumenates, classes of religious instruction, and small Christian communities are evidently places where such a catechesis can take root in the present generation and bear fruit in their lives. Only thus can we have a truly African theology and a truly African Church. Only thus can the word of God acquire a truly African flavour, so that it may reach the people of Africa.

(b) Inculturation and Theology of Liberation

African theology, it is plain, must be contextual, that is, it must take into full account the actual African situation. From what has already been said, it seems that this discipline has remained far too academic, and is for the most part irrelevant to what is going on in African society today. What are we to say of an African theology which never gets beyond the lecture halls of universities and congresses, mostly outside Africa? No one could take seriously a theology which preached the necessity of inculturation, but simply ignored the surrounding social misery. The review *Select* has taken as its watchword the criticism offered by an African student of a purely cultural Christianity: "Father, if your God is talking to us more by means of our ancestral traditions and customs rather than in the drama of four million refugees in Africa, I should like to return to you my baptismal certificate, and I ask you to cancel my name in your register. For I have no interest whatsoever in such a God!"[136]

Anyone who takes an interest in contemporary African theology can understand such bitterness. The theology of inculturation, so often preached triumphantly in African churches, is a pompous irrelevance, truly an ideological superstructure at the service of the bourgeoisie.[137] It may be a cause of some satisfaction that the African hierarchy has adopted a theology of incarnation as its official policy. So far however there have been more words than actions, and one cannot help wondering how serious is the commitment of the bishops of Africa to a truly effective incarnation of Christianity in Africa.

There are of course church organizations which are helping to mitigate the mass poverty of Africa. There have also been church leaders who have spoken out boldly on behalf of the poor. On the whole however it must be said that the church of Africa has been a silent church. Personal witness has certainly not been its strong point. It must also be said that the lifestyle of the clergy at all levels, local as well as foreign, serves to cut them off from the ordinary people. It was no foolish desire for publicity that led an African layman to address an anonymous letter to the Bishops of Africa and Madagascar, meeting in Nairobi in 1978, urging them to take the side of the poor. "If the hierarchy is to be credible as a sign of the Gospel, it must make itself so by its manner of life. When the clergy do not just save the Good News for their public professions, but live it in their own private lives, then they gain moral authority and people listen to them willingly."[138] It would be a clear sign of the Kingdom if the official representatives of the Church saved resources by vacating their huge palaces and offices, selling their no less huge motor-cars, and seeking at least to some extent to share the lot of Africa's poor multitudes. The leaders of the Church must forgo their privileges, such as the travelling

[136] Quoted by L. Mupagasi, Le lieu d'où nous confessons. Pour une théologie située, in: *Select* 7 (1982) 4. This text appears also in my: What Kind of Theology?, 125.

[137] B. Bujo, What Kind of Theology?, 125.

[138] Quoted in J.M. Ela/R. Luneau, *Voici les temps des héritiers*, Paris 1981, 205.

expenses granted by political leaders, which serve only to enslave them to governments and alienate them from the people. Bishop Kabanga of Lubumbashi expressed it thus in a pastoral letter: "We are talking about a real descent into Hell on the part of all church leaders — bishops, priests, brothers and sisters, catechists — so that we can meet our people who are still waiting there for the Messiah who will save them."[139] The Bishop is speaking of a real change of direction which the Church must take, independently of all government policies.

In the same way, African theologians too must speak with a prophetic voice. They should not begin by elaborating theories which they themselves do not put into practice. The African theologian whose real interest is personal profit cannot hope to inspire confidence. It cannot be denied that such an interest has not always been absent from the practitioners of African theology, which can only too easily become simply a valuable export. African theologians can easily turn into eager proselytizers whom you keep meeting in international gatherings but whom you never see in the bush, which should be their preferred pulpit. Many prefer to publish their studies on African theology in Europe, to catch the European and American market. Their chief object often seems to be to gain prestige and international recognition for themselves and for African theology. There must of course be dialogue with other cultures; no one would wish African theology to be practised in a ghetto. Nevertheless, it must be addressed in the first place to the people of Africa themselves, and it must be seen as a sign by the poor and the underprivileged. Theologians for their part can only too easily turn into petty bourgeois, forgetful of the poor, and concerned only with their own material advantage.

If past experience is anything to go by, the so-called African Synod which has been announced by Pope John Paul II cannot be expected to bring about renewal in the African Church. The danger is that experienced and smooth-tongued theologians will hold the stage and produce some lifeless, theoretical theology, while the voice of the poor is simply ignored.

---

[139] Kabanga, *La descente aux enfers*, Lubumbashi 1983, n. 14. cf. ibid., 18-19, n.19.

What is needed to cope with all these problems is a genuinely African ecclesiology which will produce a different model of the Church from that which is currently dominant. I shall have some suggestions to make on this matter later on, when I take up at greater length the points touched on here.

The theme of this study was the liberating dimension in African religion. It was shown how the African tradition promised salvation, and freed people for life both here and hereafter. We also saw how this tradition was shattered in the colonial period, and how African writers and theologians reacted by insisting on the necessity of recovering their lost identity. They failed however to translate the traditional dimension of liberation into the modern situation and so achieve a balanced life.

As for the incarnation of Christianity into African culture, the failure has been almost complete. There is a great deal of talk about African theology, but so far it has hardly gone beyond a preliminary clearing of the ground.

In Part Two, I shall propose models that may serve to guide further reflections and syntheses.

PART TWO

OUTLINE OF AN AFRICAN THEOLOGY

The incarnation of Christianity in Africa can only come about when it has been shown to the people of that Continent that the message of Jesus, far from destroying the liberation which traditional religion sought, provides it with a new, purifying and total stimulus. To achieve this, we must get beyond general questions, like the justification of African theology, or its aims and benefits; our task must be to bring together the fundamentals of both Christian faith and the African tradition, so that the Africans may find their own way in the resulting Christianity and feel at home therein.

The person of Jesus Christ and the community of the Church are two of the fundamentals of Christian faith. We shall examine each of them in the light of Africa's ancestor-tradition. This second part of our study deals therefore with Christology and ecclesiology from an African point of view. We shall then draw a practical conclusion, and show the consequences of Christological and ecclesiological solidarity for two particular areas of Christianity in Africa, namely, the spirituality of marriage and solidarity at the death-bed.

A. THE THEOLOGY OF ANCESTORS AS THE STARTING-POINT FOR A NEW CHRISTOLOGY

Tradition and religion have an importance in African life which may not be ignored. I shall therefore in what follows propose a Christology and trace its social and ethical consequences. Such a Christology will also elucidate the specific characteristics of the African ethic.[1]

[1] The best collection of representative views of international authors on the questions of the distinctiveness of Christian ethics, in English translation, is: Charles E. Curran and Richard A. McCormick SJ, eds., *Readings in Moral Theology*, no. 2., New York/ Ramsey 1980.

It is possible here only to touch briefly on the problem of recovering the figure of the historical Jesus. The apostles and the first Christians contented themselves for the most part with reflecting on the situation after the death of their Master, who lived and spoke as no other human had ever lived and spoken.[2] Their reflections led these first Christians to bestow upon Jesus titles borrowed from contemporary culture. These titles remained in the Christian tradition through all the cultural changes which took place down the ages.[3]

Western theologians are today calling these titles into question. They seek to speak about Jesus and about his good news in terms which modern men and women can understand. They believe that these titles, even if they originate in the Bible, are puzzling for people today and often serve to obscure rather than to illuminate the message. Christian thinkers today are striving to recover the genuinely human dimension of Jesus so that his message may really meet modern people and modern problems, instead of being wrapped in some ancient and often incomprehensible metaphysical idiom.[4]

If such a reinterpretation is necessary for Western people, it is much more urgent for those in other cultures, like the Africans, who have received Christianity in a foreign wrapping which only too often makes it impossible for them to perceive the message hidden within.

I am not able here to treat this problem in all its ramifications. I only want to say something briefly about the possibility of helping the Christian message really to enter the hearts of Africans, so that it may bear abundant fruit in a way of life which is at the same time both truly African and truly Christian. I will then consider ancestor-preoccupation as a typical, anthropocentric, African

[2] For the complex problem of the historical Jesus see a specialised bibliography. For one of the attempts at reconstruction we mention J. Jeremias, *New Testament Theology*. Part One: The Proclamation of Jesus. London 1971.

[3] E. Schillebeeckx, *Interim Report on the Books "Jesus" and "Christ"*, New York 1982, 25ff.

[4] See H. Küng, *On Being a Christian*, New York 1978. For a debate between H. Küng and W. Kasper on the legitimacy of a 'Christology from below' see: L. Scheffczyk ed., *Grundfragen der Christologie heute*, Freiburg/Basel/Wien 1975. Also E. Schillebeeckx, *Jesus, an Experiment in Christology*, N.Y./London 1979. Id., *Christ, the Experience of Jesus as Lord*, N.Y./London 1980.

"mode of thought". Before going on to offer an African- Christian model of morality, we consider Jesus as our Proto-Ancestor in whom the whole life of the African Christian can be rooted.

9. Jesus Christ as Proto-Ancestor

To grasp the problem facing us here, I may recall some essential points which I made in an earlier publication on the theme of Christ.[5]

The particular words, actions and rituals associated with the ancestors, and with the elders in general, have a deep meaning in the life of African people. They constitute a rule of conduct for the living, and they must be continually repeated. The present and the future depend on this repetition and representation of past speech, actions and rituals. It is in truth a matter of life and death. The past is enshrined in the traditions of the Fathers, but it is a past which still lives and is the guarantee of present salvation. The representation of the past in a kind of memorial calendar is no mere pious, ineffectual remembrance but a necessary return to the source of life which is essential if men and women are to be able to take a decisive step forward.[6]

We can only arrive at a true understanding of the words and actions and rituals of the ancestors when we realize that they, the ancestors and elders, have here "written down" their autobiography. Here are recorded their times of misfortune and suffering, but also their successes and joys. All these experiences constitute an inheritance handed down to their descendants. When the latter "rehearse" this inheritance, they are not only relating the lives of their ancestors but confronting their own lives with what these people did and said; they are "rewriting" the ancient autobiographies on their own account. In appropriating their inheritance, the living turn it into a source of life for the next generation.[7]

[5] See my contribution: Nos ancêtres, ces saints inconnus, in: *Bulletin de Théologie Africaine* 1 (1979) 165-178.

[6] On this see J.B. Metz, Erinnerung, in: *Handbuch für philosophische. Grundbegriffe* II 386-396. Also id., *Faith in history and society*, 184-199.

[7] For such a conception see J.B. Metz, Theology as Biography?, in: *Faith in History and Society*, 219-228. I would distinguish between 'biography' and 'autobiography', to emphasize the role of the fathers as a living testament.

It must be emphasized that this behaviour on the part of living Africans is no merely secular exercise. It is to be understood as, at bottom, part of the general framework of ancestor respect and therefore as religious. In making their acts of pious remembrance, Africans are seeking more than earthly prosperity; they are seeking salvation in its fullness. Such salvation is only possible in the measure that a person has secured it, even before death, by his or her daily behaviour. In other words, the remembering and re-enactment of the deeds of ancestors and elders is a memorial-narrative act of salvation designed to secure total community, both before and after death, with all good and benevolent ancestors.[8]

This being so, would it not be possible to develop a theology, starting out from these statements and considerations, which is capable of integrating African culture, and out of which an African Christian ethic could be constructed? More precisely, could not the recognition of the place which the ancestors and elders occupy in the life of Africans[9] stimulate theologians to construct something new? In particular, could we not use this cultural

[8] See my position on the matter of ancestors who were evil or detrimental, in my: Nos ancêtres, 173. Further id., Der afrikanische Ahnenkult, 294 and 301.

[9] See P. Kanyamachumbi, Réflexion théol. sur la religion des ancêtres en Afrique centrale, in: *Revue du Clergé Africain* 24 (1969) 421-455. J. Mawinza, Specific Difference between the Attitude toward the Ancestral Spirits and Worship of God, in: *Cahiers des Religions Africaines* 3 (1969) 37-47; the collection: *Mort, funérailles, deuil et le culte des ancêtres chez les populations du Kwango/Bas-Kwilu. Rapports et compte-rendu de la IIIième Semaine d'Etudes Ethno- Pastorales (Bandundu 1967)*, Bandundu 1969; D. Nothomb, *Un humanisme africain. Valeurs et pierres d'attente*. Préface de M. l'Abbé Kagame (Lumen Vitae, 2), Bruxelles ³1969; G. Guariglia, L'Etre Suprême, le culte des esprits et des ancêtres et le sacrifice expiatoire chez les Igbos du sud-est Nigéria, in *CRA* 4 (1970) 244-246; D. Coco, Notes sur la place des morts et des ancêtres dans la société traditionelle (Fou, Gen, Yoruba du Bas-Dahomey), in: *Les religions africaines comme source des valeurs de civilisation. Colloque de Cotonou, 16-22 août 1970*, Paris 1972, 226-237; H. Häselbarth, *Die Auferstehung der Toten in Afrika. Eine theologische Deutung der Todesriten der Mamabolo in Nordtransvaal*, Gütersloh 1972; J.F.Thiel, Die übermenshlichen Wesen bei Yansi und einigen ihrer Nachbarn (Zaire), in: *Anthropos* (St Augustin 1972) 649- 689; R. Boccessimo, Il culto dei defunti praticato dagli Acioli dell'Uganda, in: *Annali del Pontifico Museo Missionario Etnologico* 37 (1973) 9-62; Mulago gua Cikala Musharhamina, *La religion traditionelle des Bantu et leur vision du monde*, Kinshasa 1973, 29-84. P. Wymeersch, Le problème du mal chez le Muntu (Considération sur la mort et la protection contre les maléfices chez les Luwa, Bemba et Suku), in: *Africa* 28 (1973) 575-586; F. Kollbrunner, Auf dem Wege zu einer christlichen Ahnenverehrung?, in: *Neue Zeitschrift für Missionswissenschaft* 31 (1975) 19-29; 110-123. This is a very detailed report about recent attempts to 'baptize' ancestral veneration in Zimbabwe, and the theological argumentation pro and con.

phenomenon to find a new "Messianic" title for Jesus Christ and work out a new theological way of speaking of him? I would like to suggest that such a new way of speaking would be to give Jesus the title of "Ancestor Par Excellence", that is, of "Proto-Ancestor".

1. The Concept of Proto-Ancestor

To prevent possible misunderstanding, I first explain what is meant by the term "Proto-Ancestor".

We have just been speaking of community with all good ancestors. This implies that we are not taking as the starting-point of an African Christology any so-called bad ancestors, whose earthly lives cannot serve to build up, or edify, the clan or tribal community. We are not speaking of ancestors whose activities after death spread fear and anxiety rather than love among the living. When we say that we want to use the concept of ancestor as the basis of Christology, we refer only to God-fearing ancestors who exercise a good influence on their descendants by showing how the force which is life is to be used as God wishes it to be used. Only in the case of such ancestors can we speak of experiences and examples as truly a "last will and testament" left behind by the ancestors for the benefit of their descendants.

In this context, it is to be noted that the last words of a dying person, especially of a father or mother, are of particular significance. These words are words of life, setting the seal on the experiences and example of one who, while withdrawing from the community, yet truly lives on within it, along with the other ancestors. The final event in the life of a dying person is normative for those he or she is leaving behind.

If we look back on the historical Jesus of Nazareth, we can see in him, not only one who lived the African ancestor-ideal in the highest degree, but one who brought that ideal to an altogether new fulfilment. Jesus worked miracles, healing the sick, opening the eyes of the blind, raising the dead to life. In short, he brought life, and life-force, in its fullness. He lived his mission for his fellow-humans in an altogether matchless way, and, furthermore, left to his disciples, as his final commandment, the law of love.

79

The episode of the Washing of the Feet, in John 13, is of particular significance for our present purpose. The Last Supper which Jesus took with his disciples is like the final hour which a parent of a family spends with the children. He or she gathers the children about to give them a final blessing and to pronounce his or her last will. Jesus' last will was: Serve one another, love one another. Only those who carry out the terms of this will have life, and only they can transmit life to others. "If you know these things, blessed are you if you do them" (Jn 13:17).

In his earthly life, Jesus manifested precisely all those qualities and virtues which Africans like to attribute to their ancestors and which lead them to invoke the ancestors in daily life. We can therefore understand the importance of a Christology "from below" for the African context. Theology can only speak of God in human terms, and Jesus himself described God in terms drawn from human experience.[10] The legitimacy of such discourse is especially clear when we try to understand Jesus, for he is no mythical essence, to be spoken of in abstract terms, without any footing in history. Any such abstract Christology would be meaningless and would constitute an argument against the Christian faith.[11]

With this established, we can perceive the importance of Jesus for Africans in regard to ancestor-theology. This importance does not come from looking at Jesus Christ simply as an ancestor. The term "ancestor" can only be applied to Jesus in an analogical, or eminent, way, since to treat him otherwise would be to make of him only one founding ancestor among many. That is why the title "Proto-Ancestor" is reserved to Jesus. This signifies that Jesus did not only realize the authentic ideal of the God-fearing African ancestors, but also infinitely transcended that ideal and brought it to new completion. No other ancestor can be thought of who was capable of such a complete and effective realization of the ideal. This becomes clear when we consider the identification between Jesus and the imminent Rule of God, which was the

[10] See P. Hoffmann, "Er weiss, was ihr braucht" (Mt 6:8). Jesu einfache und konkrete Rede von Gott, Stuttgart 1981.
[11] See E. Schillebeeckx, The Church with a Human Face, N.Y./London 1985, 27. J. Blank, Jesus Christus/Christologie, in: Neues Handbuch theologischer Grundbegriffe, vol.3, München ²1991, 13..

heart of his proclamation. Exegetes and theologians know that "the relation between Jesus and his Kingdom-Message is not something merely external or accidental. The Kingdom was the fundamental determinant of Jesus' life and being, that which made him what he was. Everything that Jesus did, taught and promoted found in the Kingdom its final grounding. It was his own meaning."[12] All this was sealed by Jesus' death and resurrection, which validated his proclamation and the uniqueness of his Person. All that Jesus did was concentrated on the imminent Rule of God as message of salvation; from that kingdom all his acts, teaching and causes derive their meaning. It was for this same kingdom-message that Jesus died, and it was from this that his death derived its saving meaning. Through his death Jesus became the means of salvation. His resurrection also belongs essentially to the same message. It was only the Easter faith that finally made clear what was the relationship between Jesus and his God. Through the resurrection of Jesus, God brought into being a new creation, a creation which infinitely transcended the first creation, including the world of the African ancestors. Jesus Christ is the ultimate embodiment of all the virtues of the ancestors, the realization of the salvation for which they yearned. Further still, Jesus Christ is the Proto-Ancestor, the Proto-Life-Force, bearer in a transcendent form of the primitive "vital union" and "vital force". By his resurrection, Jesus is taken up once and for all into the glory of God. He not only has life, he is life, and awakens others to life (cf. Jn 11:25).

To establish a relationship with Jesus Christ, we have to keep the earthly Jesus and the Christ of faith in a kind of dynamic tension. Both dimensions must be taken into account if the implications of a "Proto-Ancestor Christology" are to be made clear. We shall then understand how Jesus, through his proclamation and through his way of living, culminating in a death sealed by resurrection, has "opened up a new relationship of human beings to God and in so doing has established a new relationship of one human being to another in the world in which they live."[13]

[12] J. Blank, op.cit, 14.

[13] E. Schillebeeckx, *The Church with a Human Face*, 30. For the significance of Jesus' resurrection see now: H. Kessler, *Sucht den Lebenden nicht bei den Toten*, Düsseldorf 1985.

2. Proto-Ancestor as Ancestor Grammar

From what has been said so far, it will be clear that giving the title of "Proto-Ancestor" to Jesus Christ is no superficial or whimsical concession to the fashion of the day. It is no mere label, corresponding to nothing in reality. My proposal has to do rather with the very essence of the Word's becoming human. To borrow the words of Karl Rahner, in the Incarnation God really assumed humanity in a decisive way. In uttering God's Word, which became our flesh, God immersed himself in the "void" of "godlessness" and "sin", so that henceforth it is impossible for us, if we wish to meet God, to ignore the man Jesus. Not to acknowledge the man Jesus is also not to acknowledge humans at all.[14] In the mystery of the Incarnation, God so truly became human that God is identified with humankind, God has become "a part of this world, part of the reality and of the history of the cosmos".[15] Since the Incarnation, human history and human time have become the time and the history of the Eternal One, and human death has become the death of the Immortal God. This implies that henceforth God can no longer be the "Unchangeable One"; God has taken changeableness. If God is the Absolutely Unchangeable, God must be able freely to assume changeability. The kenosis, the emptying, happened.[16] And it is only when God chooses to be "not-God" that the human comes to perfection.[17] This means that the human is taken up for ever into the inconceivable mystery of God, for the human can now only be conceived in relation to this God. The human person is a being whose nature it is to be continually searching for God, always on the way, ever seeking to entrust self to that ultimate mystery in which fulfilment and identity is found. This is what the Incarnation of the Word of God means. The meeting between God and humankind in this mystery is the highest stage in the realization of the human identity. Even more, since the Incarnation the human being has become "the grammar of God's possible self-expression"[18], the

[14] K. Rahner, *Foundations of Christian Faith*, N.Y./London 1978, 225.

[15] ibid., 195-7.

[16] cf. ibid., 219-227 esp. 222.

[17] ibid., 225: "When God wants to be what is not God, man comes to be."

[18] ibid., 223. Less explicitly W. Pannenberg, *Jesus — God and Man*, Philadelphia 1968, 195-211 esp. 199.

place in which God is met. What is more, Jesus Christ, the present Word made flesh, is the privileged and unique place of the total revelation of humankind. If Jesus Christ is the explanation of God, he is also the explanation of humankind.[19]

It is within this perspective that Jesus Christ is Proto-Ancestor for the African. Jesus, the Christ, identified himself with humankind, so that he constitutes their explanation. From now on, Jesus makes his own all the striving of the ancestors after righteousness and all their history, in such a way that these have now become a meeting-place with the God of salvation. Above all, Jesus Christ himself becomes the privileged locus for a full understanding of the ancestors. The African now has something to say about the mystery of the Incarnation, for after God had spoken to us at various times and in various places, including our ancestors, in these last days God speaks to us through the Son, whom God has established as unique Ancestor, as Proto-Ancestor, from whom all life flows for God's descendants (cf. Heb 1,1-2). From the Son derive all those longed-for prerogatives which constitute Jesus as Ancestor. The African ancestors are in this way forerunners, or images, of the Proto-Ancestor, Jesus Christ.[19] He is now Saviour, and the remembrance of his passion, death and resurrection must be retold down the generations, for in him is made visible in a transcendent way that future which the ancestors wish to open up to us. Their experiences become more effective in the experiences of Jesus, the Crucified and Risen One, Model of our life which makes us creative for a future to be realized on the level of salvation history.[20]

It seems to me that it is of the first importance to stress the crucial significance of this kind of discourse in African theology. Let it be said once and for all: the title of Proto-Ancestor for Jesus Christ, translated into a corresponding theology and catechesis, will have much more meaning for Africans than titles such as *logos* (Word) and *Kyrios* (Lord). It is not that we wish to suppress these latter titles. They derive however from a particular culture which Africans, in spite perhaps of the theological, exegetical and philosophical education that they have received, cannot fully

[19] See B. Bujo, Nos ancêtres, 127-173.
[20] See Mieth's article on the distinction between "example" and "model", in footnote 32 of Part One.

understand. The African's sensitivity is not touched by them, and of course the modern European or American may be in much the same situation. It is only legitimate today to give to Jesus Christ titles more deeply rooted in the culture of the people to whom the message of the gospel is being addressed. This is especially true in the case of cultures for which the conventional symbols have not even a historical significance. Edward Schillebeeckx has rightly drawn the attention of theologians to this point, observing, among other things, that the Fathers of the Church themselves called Jesus "the new Orpheus", using thus a title which would have meaning for people living in a Greek cultural and religious milieu.[21]

One advantage that I see in speaking of Jesus Christ as Proto-Ancestor is that African anthropocentrism, manifested in "ancestor-orientated" patterns of thought, is central for incarnating Christianity in Africa. The starting-point of such a procedure is in fact "ascending Christology", although certainly one may not leave out of account the indispensable elements of a "descending Christology".[22] It is important that Christianity show the Africans that being truly Christian and being truly African are not opposed to each other, because to be a true Christian means to be a true human being, since it was Jesus himself who was truly human and who humanised the world.[23] Once however we have established that the legitimate yearnings of the African ancestors are not only taken up in Jesus Christ, but are also transcended in him, can we not use the concept of Proto-Ancestor as the starting-point of a Christology for which the enthusiasm of the African will be more than a passing fashion?[24]

[21] E. Schillebeeckx, *Interim Report on the Books Jesus and Christ*, 21-7, here 25. See also his reflections about this in: id., *Jesus*, 22 and passim. W. Elligerr Orpheus-Christus, in: *Die Religion* in Geschichte and Gegenwart IV (1960) 1705.

[22] W. Kasper, *Jesus the Christ*, London 1976, 247: "Christology purely 'from below' is condemned to failure... We start 'from below' only to the extent that we reflect on the unity of God and man, even in what concerns God's side, on the basis of God's factual historical revelation in Jesus Christ". See also the studies of H. Küng (note 4 above), as well as the collection: *Diskussion über Hans Küngs 'Christsein'*, Mainz 1976.

[23] See H. Küng, *On Being a Christian*, 552. K. Rahner, *Foundations*, 226. The tendency today to start with anthropology is well demonstrated by H. Fries, Zeitgenössiche Grundtypen nicht-Kirchlicher Jesusdeutungen, in: L. Scheffczyk ed., *Grundfragen*, 36-76, esp. his conclusion on p.76.

[24] See K. Lehmann, Christsein ökumenisch, in: *Diskussion über Hans Küngs 'Christsein'*, 120.

84

The few studies on the subject do not allow us to draw firm conclusions, but neither do they contradict such a hypothesis.[25]

A "Proto-Ancestor" Christology is not the only possible model for African theology. One could also, with A. Titianma Sanon,[26] start from Jesus Christ as the Master of Initiation. Even this Christology however would bring us back to Christ as Ancestor, since traditional initiation rites derive from the ancestors, who established them as "schools of life" for their descendants. The initiate comes to new life by a kind of death and resurrection and reaches fullness of personhood.

Another Christological model might be derived from the African healing tradition. Jesus Christ might be conceived of as "Healer of Healers". This too however brings us back to the concept of life as introduced by the ancestors.

Sanon's "initiation model" contains much with which I find myself in agreement, but I would also wish to suggest that it is defective in giving the priority to the historical Jesus of Nazareth, in spite of the author's references to some New Testament texts which can only be understood in the light of post-Easter faith. A truly "incarnated" model of Jesus as Initiator must include a dimension of a "descending Christology". Indeed Titianma Sanon

---

[25] See H.W. Turner, *Profile through Preaching*, London 1965. J.S. Mbiti, Afrikanische Beiträge zur Christologie, in: P. Beyerhaus/H.W. Gensichen et al. eds., *Theol. Stimmen aus Asien, Afrika und Latein-Amerika*, vol. 3, München 1968, 75ff. — Recently, many Africans have pursued their studies on the line of an ancestral Christology, e.g. J.S. Pobee, *Toward an African Theology*, 81-98, calling Jesus 'Nana' a designation for prominent ancestors in Akan (94). He also calls him a chief (94-97). But although he speaks of the Logos and the pre- existence of the Son as Creator or co-Creator, Pobee is using continually "Jesus" as subject of such activity (85f). In any case, he is fully aware of the dangers of an undifferentiating "chief"-Christology, without being able to eradicate them (97). — See also E.J. Penoukou, Realité africaine et salut en Jésus-Christ, in: Spiritus 89 (1982) 247–267; M. Ntetem, *Die negro-afrikanische Stammesinitiation*, esp. 272-285. The models proposed by these two authors are worth considering, but although both authors state that Jesus Christ is not to be thought equal to African ancestors, they do not precisely differentiate their terminology. A different systematic proposal which is to be taken seriously is C. Nyamiti's in *Christ Our Ancestor*. Here also we find the imprecision in terminology criticised in Penoukou and Ntetem. In addition, Nyamiti calls "Ancestor" God as well as Jesus Christ, the African and non-African saints, etc. This may lead to terminological confusion, and sounds like casuistry. Nevertheless Nyamiti is logical in terms of his own system.

[26] A.T. Sanon, *Enraciner l'Evangile: initiations africaines et pédagogie de la foi*, Paris 1982. Also M. Ntetem, *Die negro- afrikanische Stammesinitiation*. E. Mveng: Christ as Master of Initiation, in: *Study Encounter*, 9 (1973) 3-5.

himself observes: "the fact that Jesus was initiated would remain nothing but a purely external example unless at the same time the act of redemption is also interpreted as initiation."[27] Sanon does not however offer any further theological reflections to bring out the deeper meaning of the Paschal Mystery.

It cannot suffice to see the initiation of Jesus as some purely external example, for Jesus was the Eternal Son of God, totally dedicated to, or initiated into, God, and he manifested that dedication in the world. The Father has the fullness of eternal life and begets the Son. They live for each other in a total and vital union, mutually reinforcing their common life. The vital power goes out from the Father to beget the Son and finally returns to the Father. In terms of the vital union of traditional Africa, there is a mutually-reinforcing stream of energy which results in the building-up of community. This vital union which produces the interaction between Father and Son, and which constitutes the bond between them, is nothing else than that divine power which, being within the Godhead, takes actual form and is identified as the Holy Spirit.

If we now come to the incarnation of God, this is constituted by the personified generation by the Father in the person of Jesus, who then transmits the life which he has received from the Father. It may be expressed thus: once initiated into the inner life of God, Jesus brings this initiation to expression in creation and lives it for the benefit of humankind. It is finally and definitively endorsed by the Father and taken up into divine glory through passion, death and resurrection. So Christ Jesus brings creation to its fulfilment and, together with the Father, leads the ancestors of the peoples of Africa into fullness of life. The Father initiates them and bestows on them a new vital energy, and a new joyful life, namely, the Holy Spirit, who unites Father and Son and now binds together in a decisive and holy unity with God the whole of creation, especially the ancestors.

Only in this way can African initiation find its place in the history of salvation. Since the time of Jesus, the vitality which initiation rites aim at transmitting is the divine life of grace, which is nothing else than the Spirit of God. All however goes back to the

[27] A.T. Sanon, *Enraciner l'Evangile*, 168.

deeds of Jesus, raised up by the Father as Proto-Ancestor and Proto-Initiator, and thereby becoming the final source of life. Through his death and resurrection, Jesus becomes the vehicle of a new life-energy, the Spirit, who unites the new clan, or tribal, community and promotes its growth.

These theological considerations have implications for Christian living. To develop a viable Christian "orthopraxis", adapted to the African mentality, it seems to me that it is a matter of urgency to work out a moral theology centred on Jesus Christ as Proto-Ancestor. The considerations which follow are proposed as general guidelines which may encourage dialogue and promote deeper reflection.

10. Jesus Christ, Proto-Ancestor, Model of African Morality

It should be understood from the outset that when we speak of Jesus as our "Model", we do not mean that he is to be regarded as a kind of prototype to be slavishly imitated. The term "model" has to be understood in the way narrative ethics uses it. Those who contemplate Jesus can find values and norms which can be integrated into their own lives so that they provide inspiration for responsible conduct.[28]

If Jesus Christ is Proto-Ancestor, source of life and happiness, our task is to bring to realization in our lives the memory of his passion, death and resurrection, making of that Saving Event the criterion for judging all human conduct. Jesus Christ becomes the sole centre of attraction, drawing all things to himself (Jn 12:32), and, through his cross, consecrating the whole of that African humanity for which the ancestors so earnestly yearned. This consecration is the goal of the absolute commitment of Jesus of Nazareth to the restoration of human dignity. He vigorously defended the rights of the weak, of women, of children, and identified himself with outcasts and sinners. The salvation which Jesus brought must not be seen simply as a revelation of his divinity;

---

[28] I. Mieth/D. Mieth, *Vorbild oder Modell?*, 110-112. In Christian ethics Imitation and Discipleship are being distinguished. See e.g. A. Schulz, Nachfolge Christi, in: *Lexikon für Theologie und Kirche* VII (1962) 758f. id., *Nachfolgen und Nachahmen*, München 1962.

Jesus emphasized that he came as Messiah in order to bring fullness of life at every level.

At the same time, Jesus insisted that the root of the matter was to be found in one's own heart. Conversion of heart: that alone can dispose men and women to receive life in its fullness. It is conversion that frees a person from the bonds of egotism and opens that person to the kingdom of God wherein alone can be found true dignity.[29] It is from this point of view that we must read the radical demands of the Sermon on the Mount. They are concerned with the relationship between human beings[30] and envisage the total humanizing of the world in the service of the Father.

From all this it follows that a reading of the gospel shows that the positive elements in African anthropocentrism are thoroughly endorsed in the person of Jesus Christ. African hospitality and sense of family; African care for the elderly, the orphaned, the unfortunate: all these things are taken up by Jesus and brought to completion.[31]

At the same time, Jesus corrects and completes the traditional morality of Africa. The moral perspective is no longer limited to my clan, my elders, my friends, but extends to the whole human race, in loving service of the Father. The morality of the disciple who accepts Jesus as Model and Proto-Ancestor is a personal re-enactment of the passion, death and resurrection of Jesus. The deeds and the moral stance of Jesus are resumed, to be remembered down the generations, giving new life to each today, and opening onto a new and fruitful future. Remembering and re-enacting the deeds of Christ constitute a liberating, "revolutionary" dynamic which can breathe new life into a dying tradition.[32]

---

[29] R. Schnackenburg, *Christian Existence in the New Testament*, Vol. 1, Notre Dame 1968, 33-66 esp. 43-50.

[30] L. Goppelt, Das Problem der Bergpredigt, in: id., *Christologie und Ethik*, Göttingen 1968, 27-43. R. Schnackenburg, *Christian Existence*, 48.

[31] See B. Bujo, African Morality and Christian Faith, in: *African Christian Morality*, 39-72. id., Kultur und Christentum in Afrika. Bemerkungen zu einem Aufsatz, in: *Neue Zeitschrift für Missionswissenschaft* 32 (1976) 212-216.

[32] On dangerous and liberating memoria see J.B. Metz, *Faith in History and Society*, 100-135. id., *Followers of Christ: The Religious Life in the Church*, New York 1978.

When Africans narrate the deeds of Christ, they are acting in complete conformity with the biblical and Christian tradition. In the Old Testament, the God of Abraham, Isaac and Jacob was revealed, not in argument or theory, but in narrative, in story.[33] The whole Decalogue can be understood as an expansion of the introductory words, I am the Lord, your God, who brought you out of the land of Egypt, out of the house of bondage (Ex 20:2; Deut 5:6). What gives the Ten Commandments their force is the memory of the liberation accomplished by Yahweh, who lives henceforth in the midst of the people. Exegetes tell us that it was the repeated recollection of the self-revelation of Yahweh which really marked and fashioned the whole character of the people of Israel.[34]

The Old Testament tradition is continued and extended in the New. It recounts the history of the Liberation, the *memoria liberationis*, begun in the Old Covenant and brought now to its final consummation in the person of the Crucified One. This *memoria* is at the same time a source of energy for the future, since the self-presentation of Yahweh before Moses, which constituted the specific Old Testament ethic, took flesh and dwelt among us, and is now the criterion of the New Testament ethic which gives a new and liberating impetus to the old history. Not for nothing was there a descent into hell (1 Peter 3:19; 4:6); the presence of the Crucified One among the dead proclaimed the liberation movement of salvation history. This liberation movement must from now on be expressed in a new experience, handed on by word of mouth from one community to another.[35] Once this

[33] On modern Christian biblical science Pinchas Lapide justly speaks of speculations which endanger the vitality of the word of God, see his criticism in: H. Küng/P. Lapide, *Jesus im Widerstreit. Ein jüdisch-christlicher Dialog*, Stuttgart/München 1976, 8f.

[34] See W. Zimmerli, Ich bin Jahwe, in: *Gottes Offenbarung*, München 1963, 11-40. G.J. Botterweck, The form and growth of the Decalogue, in: *Concilium* 5 (1965) 58-79.

[35] For a better grasp of this brief formulation, I refer to B. Bujo, Der afrikanische Ahnenkult, esp. 301-306. This article remains for the present topic decisive, — A question which interests me in respect to the descent into the underworld I formulate there: Why is this phrase applied to Jesus, even in a Creed, and what is its significance? Did the early Church have similar problems as the Africans have with their dead, to put this formula into a Creed? The exegesis of 1 Pet 3:19 and 4:6 is not very helpful. But Irenaeus, Adv hereses IV 22,2, sees in Christ's descent the liberation of all humanity, in so much as they fear God. Clement of Alexandria, Stromata VI 1 and 46, speaks of salvation available to every just person even outside of Judaism or Christianity, and

experience has been integrated, it revolutionizes history and turns into the preliminary sign of a new heaven and a new earth.[36]

It is this new perspective which must be henceforth the constitutive principle of African Christian ethics. The history of the Crucified One must be subversive for the customs and practices of both traditional and modern Africa. From the standpoint of tradition, the remembering of Jesus is a challenge to conscience, urging the elimination from life of those mistakes which might be labelled "the specific errors of African group life". The integration of the memory of the passion, death and resurrection of Jesus is a leaven which, when necessary, precisely in the name of a wider humanizing of Africa, causes certain venerable clan traditions to be abandoned.[37] This applies for example to the ideal of fertility. Turning this ideal into an absolute has often brought tragedy to childless couples, as we shall see in more detail in §13. The same ideal has often also led to the rejection of, and contempt for, priestly celibacy and to consequent discrimination against celibates (more in §12).

This discussion on the morality of the ancestors must not lead us to forget the problems which belong to "post-ancestral" Africa. I restrict my observations to certain negative features which must be called "modern African sins" and which are turning into a veritable plague. Corruption in public service is holding back human development and human progress in Africa. The same is to be said of the way authority is exercised, and of political take-overs which only mean enriching oneself and exploiting the weak. Corruption, abuse of power and the like can be overcome if Jesus Christ is given priority as Proto-Ancestor. He came so that fullness of life might prevail, but there is a pre-condition: people must agree to serve each other and show concern for human dignity. The exercise of any function, any investment with public

Origen in his Commentary to the Gospel of Matthew (III 1 ad Mt 27:50) explains it in the same way. On this trajectory the importance of Christ's descent among the dead for an ancestral Christology cannot be overlooked. — For the Descent see J.B. Metz, Redemption and Emancipation, in: *Faith in history*, 129; and esp. H.U. von Balthasar ed., *Hinabgestiegen in das Reich des Todes. Der Sinn dieses Satzes in Bekenntnis und Lehre, Dichtung und Kunst*, München/Zürich 1982.

[36] J.B. Metz, Narrative, in: *Faith in History*, 205ff.

[37] On the following see B. Bujo, Kristen-Zijn in Afrika, in: *Het Teken* 49 (1976) 163-167.

office, must be referred to Jesus Christ as model. When the first Christians gave Jesus the title of "Lord", they clearly intended to empty that title of any negative, despotic content. From now on, "Lord" excludes any master-servant relationship, for of the disciples of Jesus it is explicitly said, "it is not to be so among you" (cf Lk 22:24- 27; Mk 10:42-3; Mt 20:25-6).[38] Elevation to lordship is only possible when there is total renunciation of any exhibitionism, when humility to the point of "self-emptying" is generously accepted and made fruitful (cf. Phil 2:6-11; Mk 10:45; Mt 22:28). Modern Africans can only follow in the footsteps of Jesus Christ if they see in Jesus, not some proud tyrant, but rather the Proto-Ancestor whose last will was an appeal for human love and for untiring effort to overcome all inhumanity.

Conclusion

All our considerations on Jesus Christ as Proto-Ancestor bring us finally to the one reality which constitutes the real framework of these short reflections: the Cross. To understand Jesus as Proto-Ancestor means accompanying him on the way of the Cross. It is not enough to stand at the foot of the Cross or to gaze upon the scene at Golgotha from a distance. We are called to nail ourselves to that cross with Jesus and to suffer with him. This cross will always remain a scandal and a folly. Only the African who has been converted and has faith will see in the Crucified Jesus the Proto-Ancestor with whom he or she can identify.

Jesus is Proto-Ancestor, the eschatological Adam, life-giving Spirit (1 Cor 15:45), only because he passed through death on the Cross. It is the remembering of this event, and the retelling of it, that is both liberating and challenging. This it is which humanizes and purifies the African ethos.

I believe that a truly dynamic Christianity will only be possible in Africa when the foundation of the African's whole life is built on Jesus Christ, conceived in specifically African categories. Such an African Christocentric ethic does not of course exclude rational reflection; but to work out a theological discourse, rational reflection must be in continuous dialogue with the propositions of faith.

[38] E. Schillebeeckx, *Interim Report*, 25.

We may therefore say that we need firstly a fundamental moral theology which starts from the experiences and reflections of people in Africa, confronted with the event and coming of Jesus Christ. Such a moral theology opens the way to the development of a practical ethic by which the Africans will feel themself really challenged. This new ethic will no longer be limited to the customs of the ancestors but will also have the difficult task of addressing the modern problems of development. At the same time, confrontation with the new problems will breathe new life into the ancient customs. Only a theology which takes account of both the traditional and the modern is capable of producing an original and effective model for Christianity in Africa today.

B. THE THEOLOGY OF ANCESTORS AS THE STARTING-POINT FOR A NEW ECCLESIOLOGY

Ecclesiology cannot be separated from Christology. Questions about the organization of the Christian community can only be answered in the light of the person of Jesus Christ.

African theology seeks to use the concept of Jesus as Proto-Ancestor as the basis of a Christology. In this theology, Jesus is clearly the centre of ecclesiology, since he is seen as the founder of a new community, the community of faith.

It is on this basis that a Christological-eucharistic ecclesiology will now be proposed, orientated towards the African concept of life.

11. Christological and Eucharistic Foundations of an African Ecclesiology

The African concept of life lies behind this whole study, and it must be the corner-stone of an African ecclesiology too. Any attempt to formulate an African ecclesiology which leaves this concept out of account is in danger of remaining superficial and of talking over the heads of the Africans.

A number of suggestions were made in the first part of this study about the use of African ideas of life as the inspiration of an African Christian theology. One suggestion was that we could use the traditional concept of a clan founder to open people's minds to Jesus Christ. The notion of a "life-force" emanating from the founder and channelled from the founder to the living descendants can help people to understand Jesus Christ as a life-giver, established by God as Proto-Ancestor. Undoubtely in the Incarnation Jesus Christ, a human being like us, became a "part of the reality and of the history of the cosmos."[39] But we must think above all of the Risen Christ, of the one who, by his death and resurrection, has become a source of life for his followers in an altogether new and marvellous way.

The theme of Jesus as life-giver is central to New Testament, and especially to Pauline, theology. Paul draws a parallel between the first and second Adam (1 Cor 15:45ff; cf Rom 5:12f). and speaks of Christ as the First-Born from the dead, as the Head of the body, the Church (Col 1:18), as the First-born of all creation (Col 1:15), as the first fruits of those who have fallen asleep (1 Cor 15:20). In him resides the fullness of God, who has chosen to use him to reconcile all things (Col 1:19-20).

We may add to these Pauline ideas of Jesus as the head of creation the concept of life in the Gospel of John. Jesus presents himself as the one who has come so that his followers may have life and have it in abundance (10:10). He gives his life for the sheep, and does not behave like the hireling who abandons his sheep in the desert as soon as the wolf appears and the situation becomes dangerous (10:11,15). Jesus is the true vine, and we can only bear fruit when we remain attached to him (15:1- 6). Even more, Jesus is the Resurrection, and the one who lives in him and believes in him will never die (11:25-26). Jesus Christ is the pre-eminent source of life for the world. He is the Bread of Life and the source of eternal life (6:32-58). And so we come to the eucharistic dimension of the Church. For the Eucharist must not be treated simply as an object of contemplation. It is to be seen rather as the very life of the Church and the source of its growth.

---

[39] K. Rahner, *Foundations*, 195-8.

It is therefore clear that the African concept of Jesus as Proto-Ancestor in no way contradicts the teaching of the New Testament. It is not of course that we are treating Jesus as an ancestor in any crudely biological sense. When we regard him as the ancestor *par excellence*, we mean that we find in him the one who begets in us a mystical and supernatural life.[40]

In offering us fullness of life, Jesus offers to the people of Africa true development. After the traumas of the slave-trade and colonialism, and now the horrors of the refugee situation, the African people are searching for a new identity. Jesus Christ is our Proto-Ancestor for today, our modern Moses who will lead us through today's problems of oppression and poverty to the waters of life. In giving himself as food to those who believe in him, he becomes the life-giving grace which flows into all His descendants, the true "life-force" which Africa has always been seeking. Today the African community, clan or nation, can only develop by participating in the proto-life of Jesus, as we may call it; at the same time individuals can only help their communities to grow when they remain grounded in Jesus, the living sap which is the unique source of life for the whole Mystical Body.

When we try to construct an ecclesiology from this point of view, we see that the Eucharist as the proto-ancestral meal must be the foundation-stone of a Church which is truly African. A Church constructed on such a basis can have important prophetic consequences for the whole social and community life of modern Africa. Bahema funeral rites, already referred to, may provide an example. We have seen the meaning of the ceremony in which the sons are obliged to eat grains of millet from the hand of their dead father during the rites, and jump four times over the corpse, in

---

[40] Here I have to state a certain hesitation towards C. Nyamiti, *Christ Our Ancestor*, for example on pp. 27-28, when he insists on the biological origin of Jesus in a historical Adam, in which he sees the reason for the ancestorship of Christ for all Africans. Nyamiti himself recognized that an "Adamic" origin was not essential for Jesus' ancestral status. So our author insists on Christ's divine-human nature. It would in fact be better to avoid all arguments involving an appeal to the historical Adam, since this is a subject which raises controversy in contemporary theology. Yet I am of the opinion that the core argument for Christ's ancestorship must consist in the fact that this Christ, God-man born from God, must transcend all racial, tribal, clan-barriers in a definite way. All those who put their faith in him and are doing the will of the Father, are born of God, but not of blood or the desire of the flesh. Accordingly, Christ is Proto-Ancestor on the highest level.

94

order to call back the dead man's life-force. Both these rites have the same aim, namely, to receive fullness of life for the benefit of family and clan.

The eucharistic meal, as the basis of an African ecclesiology, must take these conceptions seriously if it is to be truly incarnated in Africa. At the Last Supper, Jesus shared bread and wine with the apostles in anticipation of his death, filling them with what had been entrusted to him by the Father, that they might find the courage to go on living and announce to the coming generation the life-giving memory and the vital power of their Lord. This memory was sealed by the death and resurrection of Jesus, which bestowed once and for all on the apostles, and on all the disciples of Jesus, the intensified proto-ancestral life-force, strengthened by the Spirit of the Crucified and Risen One. The apostles and disciples were no longer afraid to proclaim the good news and to continue the mission of their Master.

The ecclesiological model we are proposing is evidently pneumatological. We may recall here what was said above in connection with the initiation model of Christology. It was shown there how God the Father has life in fullness and, in that life, begets the Son. It was furthermore stressed that the vital power returns to the Father from the Son, so that each makes a vital contribution to the inner life of the Godhead. This interaction is at the same time itself a life-giving dynamic force which binds Father and Son in a vital unity. It was through that dynamic force, which is the Spirit, that the Father raised the Son from the dead. It is this same joyful vital power, uniting Father and Son, and constituting the inner strength of the Trinity, which now creates a new community of initiated "clan" members. The Son, raised from the dead to a new life by the power of the Spirit, is, by that same power, constituted as Proto-Ancestor. He is now the source of that power. Together with the Father, he gives in abundance the vitality which he shares with the Father, and that vitality leads the community as Church to fullness of life and eschatological completion.

This trinitarian explanation of the inner life of God corresponds exactly to the words of Jesus in St John's Gospel: "All that the Father has is mine: therefore I said that he will take what is mine and declare it to you" (16:15). If the Spirit leads into fullness of truth, this is to be understood from an African-ecclesiological point of view as an introduction to the adult life. Only one who has passed through the whole experience of the ancestors possesses the wisdom of "proven life", and consequently truth, although not truth in an intellectual sense.

On this basis, the African eucharistic celebration can be brought to life as a credible foundation of a genuinely African Church.

12. The Challenge of a Christological-Eucharistic Ecclesiology

Theoretical considerations are not enough. They must prove themselves in practice. Every member of the Church, clerical or lay, religious or secular, young or old, must go through a conversion process which will enable them to draw the practical conclusions for Africa today of the theological concept of Jesus as Proto-Ancestor, the life and the light of the post-colonial and post-ancestral Africa which must now be built on the foundations of the old. No one may shirk this responsibility.

1. Bishops and Priests in a Proto-Ancestor Ecclesiology

If the Eucharist structures the Church, and if bishops and priests, especially parish priests, have an important role in the eucharistic assembly, then that assembly itself must be rendered visible in styles of diocesan and parochial leadership. Bishops and priests have been placed at the head of the ecclesial community. Their position however is not simply one of privilege, bringing honour to the occupants. It is rather a matter of service, of *diakonia*. Bishops and priests are at the service of the ecclesial life.

We may recall that the human vocation, in the African tradition, is simply to preserve and transmit the all-embracing life which each receives from the ancestors. In every area of life, the individual has one basic responsibility: to strengthen the life of the community, be it clan, tribe or nation. If we transfer this concept to the priestly and episcopal office, we perceive that church leaders are called to deepen and to transmit to others the life of Jesus Christ, the Proto-Ancestor. Bishops and priests have the task of strengthening and deepening the ancestral life. For example every Eucharist is celebrated in union with the bishop, whether he is present or not. The bishop is named in every celebration, although always within the context of the Universal Church with which he must remain united, for he is seen as being united in a special way with Jesus, the Proto-Ancestor. On the other hand, if the bishop is not himself united with his diocese, he cannot be united with the Universal Church. The bishop should not behave as if he were the central figure of the eucharistic celebration.

Instead of praying for himself – "and me your unworthy servant" – he would do better to think of the needs of the diocesan community. The same principle applies to priests in parishes. The Mass is a celebration of parish unity, and it is perfectly proper for the parish to be mentioned in the Eucharistic Prayer.

The ideas outlined above should have an impact on the teaching and practice of the Church; they are much more than a beautiful theory. Bishops and priests have to act to strengthen the Mystical Body so that all its members may enjoy fullness of life. It is not enough for them to love their flock: they are called to give their lives for the flock in effective action.

The Eucharist should be seen really as the bread of life for Africa. But such a vision brings demands. No priest or bishop who really sees it as his vocation to communicate the proto-ancestral life in its fullness can consider his position in terms of social status. Priests and bishops who preside at the eucharistic assembly should thereby become aware of the multifarious and often crushing problems of their people. A truly eucharistic vision of ministry leads to the destruction of all clericalism and all episcopalism, so to call it, and to the abandonment of a pyramid model of the Church in which the laity are treated as mere consumers and in which the proto-ancestral life of the Mystical Body cannot circulate. We cannot honestly speak of "a living Christian community" when the laity are systematically excluded from any part in decision-making in their own Church; when decisions are taken by some clerical "fiat"; when bishops meet and take decisions affecting priests and people without consulting them, and sometimes without even informing them of the decisions. Bishops especially are in danger of regarding themselves as experts in all fields, and as above all advice, especially perhaps advice from priests, who are supposed to be their collaborators.

Some bishops are exaggerating their authority at the level of the diocese; but one may also query the attitude of many priests to their parishioners. Those outside the clerical ranks are condemned to playing a passive role, for any proposals they may offer concerning the administration of the parish are rarely listened to. The impression given is that the parish, and ecclesial life generally, is the private property of the parish priest or, at best, of all the professional religious personnel. A priest or a bishop can turn into a lifelong oppressor of the ecclesial community, effectively de-christianizing it. Priests and bishops behave like persons who cannot be corrected "from below", since their very vices and mistakes are presented as "holiness" and offered to the people as virtues to be imitated! It is clear that episcopalism and sacerdotalism, with their reluctance to engage in fraternal dialogue, constitute a kind of cancerous growth which slowly but surely chokes the proto-ancestral life. That life-giving stream which flows from the Proto-Ancestor can be selfishly monopolized by Church leaders and thus prevented from supplying the proto-ancestral Mystical Body with its indispensable nourishment.

Bishops and priests cut themselves off from their people when they do not see themselves as heirs and channels of the proto-ancestral life. How can there be any sense of solidarity with the poor and disinherited when it is taken for granted that church leaders will live in a way which is in fact in flagrant contradiction with the whole teaching of the gospel? Class distinctions will infect not just parish and diocese, but the whole of society.

The problem of class distinctions in the Church is of particular urgency in Africa, for it is there compounded by bourgeois aspirations on the part of the population in general, by dictatorship in government, and neo-colonialist pressures from abroad. It is a natural temptation for Christians to see priesthood and episcopate in terms of social promotion rather than in terms of enhancing and communicating the ancestral life of Christ. This temptation must be strenuously resisted, and a eucharistic ecclesiology can help by

98

encouraging Church leaders really to enter into the sufferings of the poor and oppressed so that they may ease them in the name of Christ. It is time to do away with a bourgeois Christianity in which the clerical office, in all its degrees, is treated as a source of material benefits, while everyone ignores the misery that dehumanizes the whole society.

It is not enough for priests or bishops in modern Africa to see themselves as spokespersons for the people and champions of the oppressed. If the Eucharist is really taken seriously as a life-giving, ecclesial meal, then Church leaders will seek to meet people where they are and to work alongside the oppressed. Bishops and priests who think it is enough to give alms to the poor are being untrue to their vocation. The Good News which they are supposed to be proclaiming summons them to strive for the eradication of poverty altogether. They must not increase the number of the poor or turn the giving of alms to these privileged brothers and sisters of Jesus into a kind of business.

How far do bishops and priests really take the side of the oppressed peasants and seek to protect them against exploiters, including Marxist exploiters, both local and foreign? How does the Church stand with regard to multinational companies and to the whole system of international capitalism, both of which pretend to be liberating Africa from underdevelopment and from the dead hand of Marxism, but in fact turn Africa into a kind of laboratory for degrading and exploitative experiments? Is our position so clear and so radical that we are willing to sacrifice our precious advantages and privileges when circumstances demand it? If not, we shall become stubborn defenders of our own titles and clerical prerogatives, accomplices in a system which despises the poor, and yet on which we pin all our own hopes for survival.

These questions are far from superfluous in a society where human beings are obliged to live in slums of indescribable squalor, while priests and bishops are living next door in bourgeois comfort. And we may surely ask if it is right to erect a vast cathedral in the middle of sub-human dwellings made of packing-cases and old tin cans. Can this be a suitable place for celebrating the Eucharist in which the Proto-Ancestor gives his life for the poor? Will not then our splendid eucharistic celebrations in Africa be more a sweet poison than the well-spring of life?

Clericalism must be rooted out of church life. But there is more to clericalism than the wealth of priests and bishops. We cannot avoid the further question of Romanism and papalism.

2. The Position of the Petrine Ministry in a Proto-Ancestor Ecclesiology

As far as I know, up to now the role of the Pope has never been discussed within the context of African theology. Yet the authority of Rome in the Church, and especially in the so-called "Third Church", means that this problem may no longer be ignored.

How then stands the question for the African Church? Here too we must refer to the ancestors. It is certainly too early to offer any final ecclesiological theory on the subject. It may however be stated in general that the African concept of life must be fundamental in discussing the Petrine ministry within the African Church.

An ecclesiology which starts from the concept of Jesus Christ as Proto-Ancestor has no difficulty in granting a privileged place both to the Church of Rome and to the successor of Peter. What has to be elucidated is the meaning of this privilege.

The Petrine ministry resembles that of the heir in the African tradition. When a son is appointed as his father's heir, he assumes responsibility for increasing the ancestral life-force among the members of his family and in the clan community generally. He must see to the just distribution of the inheritance, but he must also be attentive to all family affairs which contribute to a meaningful life for all.

An example may illustrate the situation. We have seen how Bahema sons are entrusted with their father's life-force and commissioned to use it for the benefit of the members of the family. The "eldest son" – meaning by that term "the wisest and most experienced" – has special responsibilities. It is he, for example, who inherits the family cow, although it is intended for the benefit of all. From this "sacramental" cow, each son receives a calf, representing the dead father. In these matters, the "eldest" son may not behave in an arbitrary or authoritarian manner, or deny the rights of others. His task is to be solicitous for the "sacramental" life. He is not an autocrat, but a brother among brothers.

Let us now transfer these traditions to the actual relationship between the Pope and the young particular churches of Black Africa. The Pope is like the eldest son, and the patriarchal Church of Rome is the family cow. If the eldest son tries to use all the cows and calves for his own selfish purposes, he is committing an offence against the law of life. In the context of African ecclesiology, the calves stand for the different local churches which have come of age. At first the calves stayed with the mother cow, under the leadership of the elder brother; but eventually they develop and are separated both from the mother cow and from elder brother. In the same way, Rome must grant adult rights to other local churches. On the other hand, the calves remain as representatives of the dead father and are still related to the sacramental cow which he left in his will. The new churches in the same way do not lose their link with Rome. In the Bahema tradition, the eldest son, as the steward of the mother cow, retains his mediatorial function, responsible for encouraging a good and harmonious family life, even though the other members of the family have now grown up and lead their own independent lives. He must not however meddle unnecessarily in the affairs of the other members of the family.

According to this model, an ecclesiology rooted in the African tradition would suggest that the Pope, and the Roman authorities in general, who act as advisers to the eldest son, may not interfere in the affairs of the local church in an authoritarian or paternalistic fashion. Their concern will be to foster the proto-ancestral life in the local churches so that all may develop in responsible diversity. The Pope is the eldest son, he has the presiding place. But this does not mean that he is a full reincarnation of the dead father. He must rather accept that the other brothers too have received the life-force of the same father, and not exercise his presidency as if he were the only one with a claim on the life-force which is the common inheritance of all.

101

We must therefore, in the light of these considerations, put certain questions to Rome. When we see how Rome in fact behaves towards the local churches of Africa, we may sometimes wonder whether this is really the conduct expected of a steward of the proto-ancestral heritage in the spirit of the Proto-Ancestor, Jesus Christ. Is responsible adulthood and fullness of the Christ-life really promoted in these churches? In many local African churches, one has the impression that the episcopal conference is under the thumb of the papal nuncio. The latter behaves like a ruler and pretends that he represents the Pope in diocesan matters; whereas in reality the local bishop must have more to say in local affairs than the Pope.

The arbitrary appointment of bishops in many parts of Africa is another matter of concern. Recent events have shown that this can be a problem in the USA and Europe as well, but it reaches new proportions in Africa. Apart from the fact that many European dioceses are protected by a concordat, Rome would never appoint to a European see a bishop who was from another culture or language-group. Even when Rome decided to take the appointment of Dutch bishops into its own hands, it did not appoint non-Dutchmen. And it would be inconceivable in Belgium for a Walloon to be appointed to a Flemish-speaking diocese. All over Africa however there are many examples of complete strangers being appointed to dioceses. It is evident that a bishop from another culture, and of another language, is seriously handicapped in his ministry. Often the result is almost intolerable tension between the bishop and his new diocese.

In all these matters, the impression is that Rome equates material and economic underdevelopment with religious and spiritual underdevelopment. It is at the same time evident that many African church leaders lack the confidence to take a stand against Rome, even when this is called for. One reason is clearly that such opposition would mean the turning off of the Roman tap and the consequent drying-up of funds.[41]

From the African point of view, the situation we have described means that the eldest son, the Pope, does not take

[41] On this see B. Bujo, Déchristianiser en christianisant? in: *Bulletin de Théologie Africaine* 4 (1982) 229-242. id., Au nom de l'Evangile. Refus d'un christianisme néocolonialiste, in: *Bulletin de Théologie Africaine* 6 (1984) 117-127.

seriously the life-force received from the Proto-Ancestor by his brethren, the other diocesan bishops. The further away the calves are from the mother cow, that is, the further local African churches are from Rome, the less does the Pope respect the independence and dignity willed for them by the Proto-Ancestor, Jesus Christ. Instead of being a brother among brothers, the eldest son could turn into an autocrat and betray the father.

The task of an African ecclesiology must be to call upon Rome to incarnate the Petrine ministry in the African tradition. Such an incarnation could constitute a contribution to the discussion about the papacy and could benefit the whole Church.

3. Candidates for the Priesthood and their Education

What is the situation of candidates for the ministerial priesthood in the perspective of this African ecclesiology? Many of the points raised above about bishops and priests are equally relevant in this area. A few further points may be added.

The question concerns the whole matter of priestly training. Seminaries for the education of priests are still modelled on the prescriptions of the Council of Trent. All is European: theology, spirituality, style of life. Many seminaries are still suspicious when they hear talk of African theology. In many cases the seminarians have been away from their native villages for years and have only the vaguest idea of any genuine African tradition. How can such men be expected to believe in the possibility of an African theology, or take an interest in the construction of a Church rooted in African culture?

I believe that the whole seminary course should be thought out afresh. Biblical interpretation, systematic theology, moral and pastoral theology: all should be connected with the actual situation in Africa. Even the courses in canon law and Church history should take that situation as their starting-point. On what grounds are Africans still subject to a canon law based on the European-Roman constitution and without any reference to the Black African legal situation? As for Church history, it has for centuries been expounded and interpreted by Europeans. It must today be written and taught from the African point of view.

The course of studies so far followed in African seminaries and faculties of theology must be changed. Only then shall we have candidates for the priesthood who are informed about their past and are thus equipped to come to grips with the realities of their continent. Only then will they become aware of their function in the ecclesial community as strengtheners of the proto-ancestral life.

The study of African traditions is not however in itself enough. Theory must be translated into practice. This might be arranged in the following way. Seminaries and faculties of theology are sited either in the countryside or in the cities. In either case it is important that the seminarians become familiar with the life of the people. In rural areas it is possible to bring the seminarians into contact with the village communities. They could take an interest in immediate pastoral problems as well as in agriculture, building, healthy diet and the digging of wells. One might imagine too that they could help a village family in building and cultivating. Common discussions with the villagers about all their problems would enable the seminarians to share their sorrows and their hopes. If the seminary or faculty is in a town, attention could be given to the problems of slums, prostitution, unemployment, parasitism and the like. It would truly be a pastoral ministry for seminaries and faculties of theology to accept practical work in the slums where they could look after some groups or communities and generally work for the rights of the poor and underprivileged.

Once candidates for the priesthood have really woken up to the major problems of Africa, a new kind of spirituality can be developed which situates the ministerial priesthood within the context of an ancestor theology. Then a man will only want to enter the priesthood in order to strengthen the Proto-Ancestor's life-force in all. At present African bishops boast that their seminaries are full. It is however by no means clear what is the motive which leads young people to the seminary. An attentive observer will realize that the priesthood is often treated as an instrument of social promotion. Many seminarians are obsessed with material possessions, and use their forthcoming ordination as a pretext for seeking benefactors in Europe and North America who will give them the means of living in comfort. In truth, in many African countries no citizen is as secure as the priest. He may abuse the confidence that many people, especially foreigners, place in him. So many material goods descend upon him that his basic needs of food and lodging are abundantly catered for. He knows that in the end the bishop will have to support him, and he could allow himself almost with impunity things which would never be permitted to him as a layman.

When these material advantages are placed in the foreground, it is inevitable that some people enter the priesthood as a career. Some also may see in it a position of power; after all, it may be a stepping-stone to episcopacy, where the prospects of material advantages are even brighter.

To avert this evil, Proto-Ancestor theology can provide the basis for a new spirituality which will prepare seminarians for a future ministry in which they will see themselves, not as mercenaries eager for profit, but as shepherds called to give their lives for the sheep.

In speaking of spirituality and ecclesiology, I must also offer a brief remark about priestly celibacy.

If, on one hand Africans, in the name of Jesus Christ, the Proto-Ancestor, should recommend virginity and vowed celibacy, in order to be fully integrated into the memory of the passion, death and resurrection, yet on the other hand, in the name of the same memory, they should advocate life and fertility, in so far as this does not offend human dignity, and is not erected into an absolute but is seen in the light of Easter. It is in this sense that priestly celibacy for the African needs to be examined. In fact, if Jesus did not only refuse to oppose love and fertility, which are the legitimate aspirations of the ancestors, but encouraged them; then it is not in accordance with the memory of Jesus Christ to impose as a way of life a renunciation which is in no way a narration of the saving and liberating memory of the love of Christ for the new people of God. Without falling into a monism of values which would consist in rejecting any other form of life for the sake of the kingdom of God, we must, I believe, give to African culture, which attaches great value to the experiences of the married man, the opportunity of expressing itself, and of realizing itself in the priestly life, by opening up two ways for priesthood.

I am aware that these considerations are in need of further development. They should be taken as a stimulus to further reflection.

4. Religious Orders in an African Ecclesiology

When I speak here of religious orders and religious, I include, for the sake of simplicity, also congregations and secular institutes which are not strictly religious orders. Much of what has already been said applies also to religious. Their position in the African Church deserves however special mention.

Anyone who stands for the Church and for life in Africa must also seek to promote the religious life.

It is of course possible for foreign religious orders to come to Africa and adapt themselves to the circumstances of that continent.

If however the proto-ancestral life of Christ is really to be effective in Africa, there is an urgent necessity for the founding of genuinely African, non-episcopal religious communities, that is, communities which are not founded by bishops and in a certain way controlled by them. The danger of such dependence on the local bishop is that the congregation's prophetic character will be damaged. The special prophetic charism of religious orders is that they constitute an "evangelical" opposition to the institutional, bishop-controlled church. The members of a religious order or congregation must be free vis-à-vis the pyramidically-structured Church precisely so that they may serve it by their beneficial but radical criticism. A religious who is bound to the episcopal authority, either because the bishop was the founder of the community, or constitutes its highest court of appeal, or has the right of veto in its internal affairs, has lost the freedom to speak and is in some sense in thrall to the bishop.[42]

This prophetic ministry of which we speak here is not of course to be exercised simply within the Church. It must extend to all the areas of African life. The question is, what is the function

[42] In more depth in B. Bujo, Les ordres religieux de l'époque post-coloniale en Afrique. Espérance ou déception? in: Cahiers des Religions Africaines 14 (1980), nos. 27/28, 141-150.

of religious orders and communities? It is evident that this will not be the same in Africa as in Europe or the USA. In particular, religious orders in Africa cannot close their eyes to the social problems of the continent. This means that African religious communities may not be satisfied with pursuing a purely private spiritual life of perfection which ignores the humanizing of the world and so throws overboard the mystery of the Incarnation. Since Jesus was like us in all things but sin, since he took our human nature and brought it to perfection, this human nature is no longer something secondary and inferior but belongs essentially to the domain of grace. The human can no longer be separated from the divine. The Incarnation reached its unique and once-and-for-all fulfilment in the death and resurrection of Jesus, which established him as the Proto-Ancestor *par excellence*, the unique source of life.

Once we have understood this incarnational and eschatological dimension, we shall have no more hesitation in opposing anything which deprives Africa of her life-force and leads her slowly but surely to a premature death. If African religious communities have a special task within the ancestral and proto- ancestral inheritance, their mission must be to the refugees, the shanty-town dwellers and the villagers. Genuinely African religious orders must be founded to dedicate themselves together to the basic communities of the outcasts and the deprived.

Ancient religious orders such as the Benedictines, Dominicans and Franciscans arose to meet particular needs in a particular historical context. They recognized the signs of the times. If today these communities feel the need to bring themselves up to date, how much more urgent is it to find a new and more relevant life-style for African religious communities! We should be thinking of founding new, genuinely African religious orders whose special calling would be, for example, to work with Africa's millions of refugees and do something to help to ease their terrible need. The existence of veritable palaces belonging to pitiless exploiters alongside subhuman slums must be a challenge to the Christian conscience and provoke a healthy shock which will lead to the founding of specific groups to call attention to the multiple problems of African countries. The witness, the commitment and the criticisms of such groups before an inhuman bourgeoisie would be an invaluable service to modern Africa as it searches for the ancestral life.

What has been said about town life applies also to a large extent to village communities. In modern Africa, attention to the conditions of village life would be a great blessing. Village people are neglected and handed over as helpless victims to persons of power. Farmers and peasants receive no help, while African cities cheat their people in presenting to them an illusory ideal of a European paradise. It is small wonder that the result is a massive shift of population from the countryside to the cities where over-crowding finally makes life unbearable.

It is here that religious orders could see their special function. They could make it the aim of their apostolate to make villages more habitable and life there more attractive. They could special-ize in building and help people to construct healthier and more comfortable houses. They could become experts in agriculture and animal husbandry, and thus be in a position to offer villagers practical help in this vital area of their lives. They could seek to restore ancient handicrafts which are rapidly being forgotten. They could influence market prices by their products and by their commitment, and defend the rights of the peasants. Religious should also take to heart what was said about the work of semi-narians in making people aware of the importance of hygiene, especially clean water and a healthy diet. With all this, the religious orders would also tackle the phenomenon of illiteracy and collect and promote the elements of African culture, including religion, customs and manners, music, and art in general.

Only when these tasks are taken seriously can Africa recover its youth and its dynamism. African religious must wake up to their responsibilities. They must see the eucharistic meal as the proto-ancestral meal, the source of life both in time and in eter-nity. When they draw the consequences of this perception, they will cause the ancestral and proto-ancestral life to flourish for the benefit of the whole Mystical Body of the Proto-Ancestor.

5. The Task of the Missionary within the Mystery of the Proto-Ancestral Body

A modern African ecclesiology cannot avoid considering the position of missionaries in the African Church today.

In the African tradition, it will be recalled, the life of a stranger is to be respected; the stranger must be received with generous hospitality. An outsider can even become a member of the host's family or clan, by means, for example, of the blood pact.

According to these principles, the missionary who comes to Africa in the name of Jesus Christ is not a stranger. For the African Christian, the missionary is simply a member of the Mystical Body of the Proto-Ancestor who, by the blood of the Cross, and by the Holy Banquet, fashions all into one body. All belong by equal right to the clan of the Risen One.[43]

This theological basis of the work of foreign missionaries in Africa has far-reaching practical consequences. The Africans should not see them as foreign whites but, without prejudice, as brothers and sisters in the same proto-ancestral clan. They should not be regarded with suspicion, as if their object were to deprive Africans of the best pieces of cake. As members of the proto-ancestral family and clan community, they have the right to spend their old age in the place where they have worked all their lives. They should not be shipped back to Europe, where they may no longer have close relatives, to while away a lonely old age. Many missionaries have been the pillars of our church; they should be buried in our soil and venerated as leaders of the Church.

Africans then have obligations to missionaries. Missionaries, on the other hand, must recognize their basic obligation to conduct themselves like trustworthy blood-brothers and sisters of Africans. There are unfortunately missionaries who come to Africa with preconceived notions of educating uncivilized people. It is the case that some of them treat an African diocese like a piece of cake which they can share out as they please without reference to the African clergy. Such persons refuse to accept that they are in

[43] What is here claimed for expatriate missioners, may be applied to African tribal and clan communities: they all are brothers and sisters in the Proto-Ancestor.

fact guests of the African clergy who have admitted them into fellowship under the same Proto-Ancestor, and with whom they are called to enter into fraternal dialogue for the benefit of the whole Mystical Body.

Of course missionaries differ. One may perhaps distinguish three sorts. Some devote themselves without reserve to the welfare of the local church. These are a small minority, and for the most part they are regarded by their colleagues as a nuisance and even as traitors. A second group, the majority, take refuge in silence and refuse to take sides in current disputes. They think that this makes them impartial, but in fact their silence may often amount to a blameworthy taking of sides.[44] A third group behave unashamedly like masters and are concerned only with the interests of their own religious family. They have a wide influence and alienate the local people.

It is impossible to avoid the impression that many missionary congregations want to prolong their stay in so-called mission lands indefinitely. They may indeed have set on foot useful projects which they still administer. But one must ask why they continue to occupy key positions in a number of dioceses when these could be handed over to the local clergy. They often avoid training local successors, on the grounds that no one is competent to succeed them. Occasionally there may be substance in this contention, but it can happen that a local person has all the necessary qualifications, but is still classed among the incompetent. Missionaries should examine their consciences on this matter, and ask if they are always sincere and truthful, or if they have not for a long time turned what should be a fraternal relationship into that of master to servant.

The power of the missionaries is discernible especially in the appointment of bishops, for it is to the opinions of the missionaries that Rome pays special heed. The missionaries tend to exploit this situation by recommending candidates who will be obedient to them. However unsuitable a candidate may appear to the local people, and even to the missionaries themselves, if he abstains from criticism of the missionaries, however justified, he stands a good chance of being appointed. The object of this be-

[44] A. Boesak, *Farewell to Innocence*, New York 1977.

110

haviour seems to be to secure for the missionaries a base and permanent home in Africa, where they can continue to indulge their taste for power in the name of the faith. Yet if the Bible is taken as guide, according to the tradition of Abraham, missionaries should be without abode, trusting in God alone.[45] This clinging to an unbiblical, and unevangelical, domestic security is evident, for instance, when a bishop, whom I can only call a missionary yes-man, is thoroughly spoiled, along with his diocese, while one who refuses to be compliant finds his diocese starved of funds. Thus the African church is turned into an instrument for the convenience of missionaries, swimming in their wake and ministering to their interests. Lay people rarely criticize the system, but a priest who ventures to do so incurs the hostility of the missionaries, and may find himself labelled a "Marxist", with all its unpleasant political consequences.

Missionaries must stop behaving like neo-colonialist bosses. They must be, not oppressors, but liberators, who bring good news. If they are to win a welcome for their message, they must study deeply the culture of their new homeland and seek a truly fraternal relationship with the local people. Only then can their word really take flesh and contribute to the advance of the proto-ancestral life, and only then can we have a truly African church.

6. The Contribution of the People to the Proto-Ancestral Life

The proto-ancestral Mystical Body does not exist for its own sake, neither is it something static, for it is realized in a continual dialectic of give and take. We have spoken so far of bishops, priests and religious. But of course we may not lose sight of the great mass of other people who make up the Mystical Body.

As far as the ordinary people are concerned, many examples could be offered to show how each has responsibility to advance the values which promote the spread of life and so enlarge freedom in all the areas of human activity. We have already noted how care is needed lest the traditional virtue of hospitality, for example, be abused and transformed into parasitism. Another ex-

[45] See on this J.B. Metz, *Den Glauben lernen und lehren. Dank an Karl Rahner*, München 1984, 24-26.

ample of the same kind may be given. The real meaning of African solidarity is to be found in the building up of the ancestral Mystical Body. Today however this solidarity is wrongly understood, and it becomes an instrument of oppression. People in influential positions use their power to procure exclusive privileges for their own kinspeople and clan community at the expense of outsiders. It often happens that doctors are really only interested in their relatives, and may demand extortionate bribes from people they do not know. Politicians may channel development to their native villages or districts when other areas are in much greater need.

All these modern diseases are eating away at Africa like a cancer. It is true that in the African tradition everything was concentrated on the good of the clan community. But the tradition did not exclude a wider perspective. On the contrary, members of the clan were expected to concern themselves unreservedly also with strangers, for these too had the right to increase of life.

To return now to the Christology outlined above, Jesus Christ, the Proto-Ancestor, eternally born of the Father, is the founder of a new clan community. The members of this new clan are all who believe in his name, "who were born, not of blood nor of the will of the flesh nor of the will of man, but of God" (Jn 1:12-13).

Membership of this clan makes demands far more radical than the old clan loyalty. We are called now, not just to show hospitality to passing strangers, but to extend our benevolence to all other human beings without distinction. In the modern situation, one's sense of solidarity may not be restricted to the members of one's own nation, but must extend, for example, to other African countries where people are oppressed by various miseries, such as want, famine, war and dictatorship. We Africans should be ashamed of waiting for more highly-organized countries to help our suffering neighbours when we could quite often come to their rescue ourselves. We do not seem to feel any sympathy for our suffering fellow-Africans who are oppressed by Marxism, capitalism, racism, imperialism, and so many other "isms". South Africa may also be cited in this connection. We were accomplices in apartheid by our silence, and by leaving protests to Europeans and North Americans.

112

While confronting vigorously the sufferings and cruelties of African countries, we must not forget those other people, perhaps far away, with whom we are joined by faith and Eucharist. Our sense of solidarity must extend beyond Africa to all the suffering peoples of the world, in Asia and Latin America, for example.

When we speak of the responsibility of the people of God, we cannot help thinking in particular of African leaders, especially when they are Christians. True leaders must not think of their own interests, but must be dedicated to increasing life throughout the community. This ancient African tradition is crucial for modern Africa. Chiefs must exercise their authority, not for their own benefit, but for the sake of all. The chief has no right to operate as a kind of lone ruler, apart from the people. Frequently the people would depose and unsatisfactory chief, all the more reason for a leader to work with the people.[46]

We saw when speaking of Christology how the demands of Jesus Christ, Proto-Ancestor, go far beyond the demands of any traditional system. Often the new community must contradict the ways of the old. So in former times a traditional chief might seize the property of a subject and appropriate it.[47] Such traditions are wrong, springing as they do from a lust for power, and spreading, not life, but craven fear. Jesus Christ sweeps them away.

The role of the ordinary people is indispensable in building up the Church in Africa. The leaders of this ecclesial community should make use of a suitable catechesis to help everyone to play their part in bringing about a community which is ever more creative and forward-looking, and a vibrant sign of the health of the eucharistic assembly.

Conclusion

An ecclesiology which is really to speak to the people of Africa must be grounded in the concept of life. We have tried to show also how an African ecclesiology must be rooted in a theology of

---

[46] If traditionally in many tribes chiefs could be deposed for inefficiency, this may be the case for politicians, and even for bishops and parish priests. They have to give account of their ministry.

[47] E. Mujynya, *Le mal et le fondement dernier*, 73f.

Christ and of the Eucharist. In particular, it may not grant to canon law the large place which some African bishops would like it to have. A Church founded on canon law would be a bloodless and lifeless thing. Only when we give the primacy to Christ and the Eucharist, and relegate canon law to its proper, secondary place, can we make our own the words of the New Testament:

> Something which has existed since the beginning,
> which we have heard,
> which we have seen with our own eyes,
> which we have watched
> and touched with our own hands,
> the Word of life -
> this is our theme.
> That life was made visible;
> we saw it and are giving our testimony,
> declaring to you the eternal life,
> which was present to the Father
> and has been revealed to us.
> We are declaring to you
> what we have seen and heard,
> so that you may share our life.
> Our life is shared with the Father
> and with the Son Jesus Christ.
> (1 Jn 1:1-3).

C. AFRICAN CHRISTOLOGY AND ECCLESIOLOGY ON TRIAL — TWO CONSEQUENCES

Christology and ecclesiology have been presented as dimensions which must permeate the whole of Christian life. To make this proposition clearer, I choose two examples which seem to me to be of great importance in Africa. These are a spirituality of marriage and care for the dying. The first will be considered in the context of an African Christology and the second more from the point of view of ecclesiology.

13. A Spirituality of Marriage for Africa

The African understanding of marriage is undoubtedly to be numbered among those customs and usages which must be integrated into the Christian tradition to help towards the creation of a genuinely African Christianity.

Marriage is a burning issue for the Church in Africa today. We cannot treat all the details here, but it will be of interest to give the results of some contemporary research before offering tentative suggestions for a spirituality adapted to current difficulties.

Remarks about creating an African spirituality are not meant to replace ethical reflection. But in a milieu in which ethical rules are formulated on the basis of religion, preliminary research can provide many useful indications for solving the problem of marriage.

1. The African Tradition within the Christian Context

When marriage is discussed in Christian circles in Africa, the subject of "trial marriages" nearly always crops up as a major stumbling-block. The reason for this is that, in African society, the achievement of life, as commanded by the ancestors, is an affair of the whole community. In the societies of Africa, a man who dies childless falls into oblivion. He will be unable to find happiness in the next world because, having no children to honour him, he is cut off from the family community. Some tribes place a piece of charcoal in the mouth of a man who has died childless, apparently

115

to signify the final extinction of one who has left no issue in whom he might continue to live.

Childlessness is a personal disgrace. It is also felt as a kind of slur on the community, a social fault, and it often leads to divorce or polygamy. It is therefore understandable that many tribes expect their members to enter marriage on a provisional basis until the wife's ability to bear children has been established.[48]

What should be the attitude of an African Christian to such customs? The Christian pastor is confronted with the difficulty of how to prevent Christian converts, or those who have grown up in the faith, from being totally cut off from the tradition of their tribe.

Experience has shown that a marriage which has been validly celebrated in church, but without regard to the traditional customs, is essentially fragile, especially if it remains childless.

Many theologians have tried to tackle this problem, and various solutions have been proposed.[49] The solution which many now favour, and which seems likely in the end to prevail, is that church discipline must be relaxed so that African partners may live together before marriage.[50] This refers especially to the discipline of the Roman Catholic Church. Some have even suggested that the African view of marriage should be extended to the universal church, so that infertility would be everywhere an impediment to valid Christian marriage.[51]

---

[48] Admittedly, there are other reasons for a trial marriage, e.g. mutual knowledge, yet the testing of the fertility of the woman remains the main motivation. See D. Vandenberghe, Contribution à la pastorale du mariage en Afrique, in: *Orientations Pastorales* (=OP) 119 (1968) 221-254. L. Mpongo, Le mariage chrétien en Afrique noire, in: *OP* 120 (1968) 313-333. id., L'infécondité comme empêchement dirimant?, in: *Revue du Clergé Africain* 24 (1969) 696-711. On the question of fertility, Mulago gwa Cikala Musharhamina, *Traditional African Marriage and Christian Marriage*, 58, says: "In African marriage the aspect father-mother is more important than the aspect husband-wife".

[49] Besides the bibliography in note 48 see A. Hastings, *Christian Marriage in Africa*, London 1973. B. Kisembo/L. Magesa/A. Shorter, *African Christian Marriage*, London 1977. M. Legrain, *Mariage chrétien, modèle unique?* Paris 1978. Boka di Mpasi Londi, Le mariage prend le maquis, in: *Telema* 15 (1978) 3f. id., Inculturation chrétienne du mariage, in: *Telema* 17 (1979) 3f.

[50] Even in the last decade R. De Haes, Recherches africaines sur le mariage chrétien, in: *Combats pour un christianisme africain*, Kinshasa 1981, 33-43. Response by B. Bujo, Notes complémentaires à la contribution de R. De Haes sur le mariage africain et chrétien, in: *Combats*, 45-49.

[51] See F.M. Lufuluabo, Mariage coutumier. Contrary position L. Mpongo, L'infécondité comme empêchement dirimant?

116

Not everyone of course is in agreement with this position. Apart from L. Mpongo,[52] one may refer especially to the Colloquium on African Morality in Kinshasa in 1969,[53] and to the Theological Week in the same city in the following year. Both of these gatherings insisted that the Church had no right to offer to Africa a "cut-price" Christianity. The Church's task everywhere was to proclaim and maintain the Christian ideal; she was not empowered, it was maintained, to water it down to suit circumstances, but was commissioned to educate the faithful to the demands of the gospel.

This position seems both too severe and too sweeping, and we can understand the complaint of Walbert Bühlmann that the Kinshasa Theological Week had reverted to an earlier theological position.[54] The gospel of course remains normative, but we may not simply ignore the needs of married people.

At the same time, Bühlmann is perhaps too uncritical in siding with the defenders of trial marriage. He seems to belong to that varied school of theologians[55] who, while expressing themselves differently, and seeking to avoid open confrontation,[56] are all anxious to dispose of the proposal of Vandenbergh and Lufuluabo that we should speak of "marriage by stages" or "marriage by steps", instead of using the more direct expression "trial marriage". What these writers mean by marriage by "steps" or "stages" is a process of instruction, like the stages of a catechumenate, in which engaged couples are accompanied by the church along the traditional steps to marriage, which are thereby recognized by the Church as legitimate.

---

[52] L. Mpongo, L'infécondité, and the studies quoted in note 48.

[53] See Ethique chrétienne et valeurs africaines, in: *Cahiers des Religions Africaines* 3 (1969) 154f.

[54] W. Bühlmann, *The Coming of the Third Church*, London 1976, 313.

[55] E.g. Mulago gua Cikala Musharhamina, *African Traditional Marriage*. R. De Haes, Recherches africaines. W. Bühlmann, Fragen zur Ehe und Familie. Bringt 'Familiaris Consortio' die Antwort? in: *Theologie der Gegenwart* 25 (1982) 159-171.

[56] Even if Bühlmann in *The Coming of the Third Church*, 313, mentions the Theological Week of Kinshasa, he is only reporting but not arguing theologically. The position of L. Mpongo is not reported, and the Colloquium of Kinshasa on African ethics 'Ethique chrétienne et valeurs africaines' is nowhere quoted.

This attitude can be discerned in the statements made by African Bishops during the Roman Synod of 1980.[57]

What still remains to be clarified however is what precisely are these "stages" which are to precede, or even to constitute, marriage. Some evidently think that it is not just a matter of giving a couple the time to get to know each other but of "legitimising" sexual cohabitation. In this connection, Bishop Kaseba of Zaïre presents marriage as a series of stages: "It is a matter of a life process that goes ahead step by step and no stage can be left out. As the catechesis for baptism leads progressively to baptism, so with the catechesis for marriage. One should not speak of "premarital" relations. They already belong to marriage proper, which takes place not in a momentary ceremony but is accomplished in a gradual process."[58]

One may however wonder whether this is the correct theological approach to the problem. It may not constitute the solid foundation which Bühlmann finds in Bishop Kaseba's contribution.[59] Is there no other way of helping Africans in their married life? It seems to me that there has not been enough theological reflection on this delicate subject so as to decide so hastily in favor of "trial marriage". The following reflections are intended as a further contribution.

2. Outline of a New Spirituality

The solution to the problem of trial marriages given above seems to me to be one-sided and generally unsound, principally because it does not take into account the situation in the whole of Black Africa.

Even when people recognize that there are different cultures in Africa, they may still fail to realize that quite different tribes may still live side by side, so that some kind of uniform pastoral

---

[57] See periodical AFER, Special double issue on the Synod of Bishops 1980, Eldoret/Kenya, February to April 1981. In addition we are in possession of the votes of East African bishops at the Synod: 'Family Life today', unpublished.

[58] AFER (See note 57) 40f, quoted by W. Bühlmann, Fragen zur Ehe und Familie, 163.

[59] W. Bühlmann, Fragen, 163.

approach is necessary.[60] We urgently need a comparative study of African marriage customs to provide the foundation for pastoral practice. It is true that fertility is everywhere important, and that everywhere too in Africa marriage takes place in a series of stages. At the same time, I would object to Bishop Kaseba that there are many peoples who know nothing of "trial marriages" involving a premarital sexual relationship. In some tribes, the young man was allowed to take his prospective bride with him to his parents' home for a time, but sexual relations were forbidden under pain of severe punishment.[61] When it was a question of determining the sexual capacity of the young people, there were ways of finding out which stopped short of intercourse. What is more, a man might take a second wife if the first wife proved infertile, but the latter still remained his wife.[62]

Anyone who wants to introduce a new form of Christian marriage in Africas should not exaggerate the comparison between African trial marriage and earlier Western models of marriage simply to convince the Roman authorities, for example, of the legitimacy of the proposals referred to above.[63] The local church should proceed by comparing different African marriage-customs and seeing how they can be made fruitful for each other. Only thus can a genuinely African solution to the problem of marriage be found. More particularly, for our purpose here we may ask why it is that some tribes have been able to accept the Church's marriage-laws without any difficulty or sense of disruption. The explanation must be that these laws already found a grounding in the tribal tradition. The question is, how did some tribes come to develop such customs? There needs to be a dialogue between tribes with different marriage traditions. The undertaking would not be easy, and it would be some years before everything was clarified. The alternative to venturing along this path, however, is simply to take the existing rules as normative.

---

[60] Also ibid., 162-5, not taking account of this aspect.

[61] See Pilo Kamaragi, La sociologie des institutions matrimoniales chez les Bahema de Djugu (Zaire), unpubl. dissertation Rome 1982. Different from the Baluba of Kasai (Zaire): Mulago gwa Cikala Musharhamina, *Traditional African Marriage*, 35f.

[62] Such polygamy implied high ethical demands which would be refused by many today. See more by B. Bujo, Die pastoral-ethische Beurteilung, esp. 178.

[63] See for example the studies mentioned by Mulago and De Haes.

This does not imply that the pastor may not use discretion in judging particular situations. It is not only possible but necessary to exercise a broad tolerance, for pastoral and pedagogical reasons, until the present phase of uncertainty has been overcome.[64] If the Church were to proceed arbitrarily to institutionalize trial marriage, this would be an offence to tribes which do not practise it. It would in fact give the impression that the Church disapproved of the ban on premarital congress and was advocating a practice "that is not found even among the pagans"(1 Cor 5:1).

The only way out of the impasse is to find common ground among all the tribes of Africa. Such common ground can be found in an ancestor theology, for the foundations of such a theology are found everywhere. Everywhere the African tribes revere their ancestors. Undoubtedly an ancestor spirituality would be a great help to the African in the moral problems of daily life.

When Africans turn to Jesus Christ, the Proto-Ancestor, they find in him a model of dedication to the community, unfailingly on the side of the weak and the despised. These were the ones with whom he identified Himself, becoming one with them so that all might share in the glory of God. When they bring their marriage problems to Jesus, they can see at once that African attitudes must change, and especially the attitudes of African men. The African male needs to make his own the last will and testament of the Lord, abandoning all pretensions to superiority and turning in love to a barren wife; for she is to be numbered among the weak ones who were especially dear to Jesus. She enjoys the fullness of life which flows from the Proto-Ancestor, and may not be treated simply as a bearer of children. As a child of God and a kinswoman of Jesus, she has worth in herself. To treat a woman, or indeed for that matter a man, simply as a source of children is to degrade them to the status of objects whose only worth is in their productivity. It is an example of that same achievement mentality which the African vehemently condemns in the industrial nations. Even if the ancestors made fertility a necessary condition of marriage, the baptized African must understand that, while it cannot be denied that Jesus Christ endorses the African world-

---

[64] B. Bujo, Notes complémentaires, 46f.

view on the whole, he corrects its negative points. If the memory of the passion, death and resurrection of Jesus Christ, the Proto-Ancestor, is truly to be a leaven in African society, then certain traditions, however venerable, must be abandoned. If they damage human dignity, they are in fact in opposition to the basic mind of the ancestors, which was to open the way to a more human future and to a more complete life. Those who want to be faithful to the fundamental intention of the ancestors should make the narration of the story of Jesus into the criterion of African ethics. The African spouse cannot leave out of account the fact that the memory of Jesus Christ has nothing to do with prestige, and that rising to glory is only possible by the way of the Cross. What may have been allowed or tolerated in traditional society is for ever superseded in the memory of Christ and in the descent into hell, where the presence of the Crucified One finally uplifted all customs and usages. Thus childlessness or infertility, which were considered as evil and as a disgrace to society, have to be placed by the Christian under the sign of the Cross, so that love, and not having descendants, becomes the foundation of the marriage communion.

These suggestions for a new spirituality do not only apply to married couples. They are also relevant for the whole tribe or clan which, by its rejection of childless marriages, leads married people to betray the promises they made to each other. Reference to Jesus Christ as Proto-Ancestor could change this mentality and purify this attitude.[65]

3. Final Considerations

We have spoken of the necessity of a spirituality which takes into account the African background. A central feature of that background is religious. Knowing no distinction between "world ethos" and "salvation ethos", the African's whole world is religious, as has often been noted. This does not contradict however the attempt in Africa to elaborate a rationally-based morality, especially when we think of the many intellectuals who

[65] On this whole question B. Bujo, Die christologischen Grundlagen einer afrikanischen Ethik, in: *Freiburger Zeitschrift für Philosophie und Theologie* 29 (1981) 233 and 235.

121

have been deeply influenced by modern secularism. In spite of the campaigns for authenticity in many countries, the more educated people are not convinced by any argument from mere authority, including the authority of the ancestral tradition. They are increasingly demanding to know the reasons for rules of conduct, whether Christian or traditional. At the same time, it is interesting to observe how selective people can be in deciding which rules to prefer. As far as marriage, for example, is concerned, educated young women are not prepared to accept the idea of trial marriages to test fertility. They may be willing to become a second wife, but they still nourish the hope of becoming a man's only wife and not some kind of temporary partner. Educated men on the other hand appear more willing to accept traditional ideas on fertility, along with the tradition of male domination, although this derives essentially from the rural situation.

It is the task of African moral theologians to lay foundations. They have to provide a moral education that takes into account the experiences of the people. A proper moral catechesis for rural people, who form the real cradle of the leading social class, needs to be elaborated, taking into account their deeply-felt, ancestor-based religious feeling. Only when this preliminary work has been completed will the way be clear for rational moral debate.

It is remarkable how little attention has been paid to the necessity of this preparatory work in discussions about African marriage. Bishops and theologians need to wake up to their responsibility for developing a well-founded spirituality of marriage, instead of sheltering behind a tradition which is not accepted by many of the tribes of Africa. We need a common basis, rooted in ancestral spirituality, and centred on Jesus Christ as Proto-Ancestor. Further research is urgently needed to establish such a basis.

14. Death and Care for the Dying in the African Context

The treatment of the dying is central to medical ethics. It is becoming clearer every day that it is not enough to perfect medicine as a physical science: the whole of the patient's context has to be taken into account. It is however far from easy to realize this ideal. As understanding progresses in what it means for a human to be a body-spirit compound, the question becomes more insistent: How can I offer appropriate help to a person facing death? Is it reasonable to go on prolonging the life of one who is enduring agonizing pain? Would it not be better to give a lethal injection? Is it not an offence to human dignity to prolong life by artificial means when only a vegetative life is possible, or when the inevitable death can only be postponed for a few hours or days?

During my time in Europe, spent for the most part in Germany, I could not avoid encountering some typical contemporary Western problems, such as loneliness, chronic illness, old age, adjustment to death. This experience naturally led me to reflect on my own society at home, in which human relationships to some extent form a different pattern. I would like in the final section of this book to speak of African attitudes to death, not in order to instruct Europeans, but to warn Africans of the dangers which lie ahead from the progress of medical science. Without condemning scientific progress Africans must beware of abandoning their traditional values in favour of purely materialistic solutions to the problems of sickness and death.

1. The Religio-Human Dimension

Europeans are often surprised by the matter-of-fact way in which Africans seem to accept death. A. Van Soest writes of a fairly typical experience: "During my ministry in Ghana, I was summoned one evening to a village chief who, I was told, was dying. When I arrived, I found a meal in progress, with all the dying man's sons, as well as his councillors, seated round the table. The dying man himself was at the head of the table, hardly eating, but bidding farewell to his sons and thanking his councillors for their help. Finally he retired to his hut, and we all left. About two o'clock in the morning, the sacred trumpets rang out to announce that the chief had died a half-hour earlier. Everything had been done properly and in good order."[66]

---

[66] A. van Soest, Erfahrungen mit Sterbenden in Krankenhäusern, in: P. Dingwerth/H. Tiefenbacher, eds., Sterbekliniken, oder Was brauchen Sterbende?, Stuttgart 1980, 23.

Such behaviour is not uncommon, and it is to be explained by an underlying attitude which is both religious and communitarian, as described in the first part of this book. Community is a central African value. This community is not restricted to the living, but includes the dead members also. The basic idea is of sharing, of partnership, which, in the context of African theology, I have called vital union. Every member of the community, whether it be family, clan or tribe, knows that he or she only lives by the life of the whole, and that God and the Founding Ancestor are the sources of that life.

Dying people therefore are conscious that they participate in the life-force of the ancestors. There is no question of despair in the face of death, and no sense that one is being deprived of life. The dying African, especially one in authority, who is conscious that he or she has lived a life according to traditional rules sets out on the journey to the land of the ancestors in full confidence that he or she will be received into their community.

The task of the living is to help the dying on their way. In many tribes it is the custom to place coins in the hand or mouth of the dead, in amounts appropriate to their position in the community. These coins are to be interpreted as his "fare" to the next world. Sometimes too the dead person is given "weapons, tools and the symbols of his rank and dignity".[67]

It is believed that these services to the dead make possible a happy future with the ancestors. It was the custom in Rwanda to place in the hand of the dead person one or two leaves of the Erythrina tree. This tree had a sacred character. According to legend, Lyangombe, the blessed of God and the Hero in charge of the dead, was wounded by a buffalo and carried under an Erythrina tree to die. Connecting the dead person with the leaf of this sacred tree symbolized the special bond with the ancestors.[68]

Of course the African fears death, in common with all human beings. The person is however to some extent reconciled to the fact of death by the belief in the community of the ancestors in which he or she is destined to live. "He must not only move to the land of the ancestors, but must be accepted and given a place

[67] J, Theuws, Death and Burial in Africa, in: *Concilium* 32 (1968) 140-143, here 142.

[68] See M. Pauwels, Usages Funèbres au Ruanda, in: *Anthropos* 48 (1953) 30-43.

there."[69] Africans also know that they will remain linked with the community of those they are leaving behind. Alongside these religious convictions, the dying person is also helped by practical assistance from the whole clan community.

2. The Support of the Clan Community

Two points may be here considered: firstly, the experience of death in Africa; and, secondly, the final farewell.

(a) **The Experience of Death in Africa** The reality of death comes home to Africans from their earliest years. Often enough a child's very name will suffice to keep the prospect of death permanently before the mind's eye: Kufa-Lobi (you die tomorrow); Bbûdhe (candidate for death tomorrow); Dhedonga (Death knows no shame); Dhehwilete (Death will not spare you).

In a traditional African home, people are of course much more in contact with death than are people in societies with an abundance of hospitals and undertakers. Even today, people in Africa rarely die in hospital. Friends and relatives really accompany the dying on their last journey. In a sense, they share the dying. The corpse, instead of being hurried off to a mortuary, remains in the home until the time for the solemn burial, probably after about two days. The custom of keeping the dead body at home naturally has an influence on people's general attitude to death. In Christian families, the home of a recently-deceased person becomes a kind of holy place where people pray and read from the Scriptures. Here, face to face with death, priests, catechists, members of the family and clan, take turns to preach. This vigil might last from half a day to two full days. In this way people tried to cope with death and integrate it into their life. How far this integration was successful may be seen at the death-bed, not only as regards the dying person but also as regards those who accompanied that person.

(b) **The Last Farewell** Traditional African thought did not divide the human person into body and soul. This philosophy of the person as a unity had repercussions on the practice of medicine. It was not considered enough to treat a particular organ

[69] See J. Theuws, Death and Burial, 142.

125

or member, for it was the whole person that was sick. The traditional healer would pray for the patient before administering herbal remedies,[70] over which also was invoked the blessing of God and the ancestors. Treatment would be carried out in the presence of the family, thus reflecting the sense that the human is essentially a social being, as well as a unity of body and soul. Rituals and dances were performed to restore the body–soul equilibrium which the illness had disturbed. Traditional healers attributed importance to skin-contact, and they would supplement their physical treatment by laying hands on the sick person and offering the person words of comfort. They might also prepare a special dish and feed the person as though a child.

The patients were often not told of the seriousness of their condition but left to find it out for themselves. When the healer had exhausted his resources, and there was no improvement, the sick person might ask to be left to die in peace, or the family might make the request. In the modern situation, a patient who recognizes that his or her condition is hopeless may ask to leave hospital and go home to die among his or her own people.

What then can we say about help to the dying in traditional Africa? If adult persons think that their death is approaching, they must tell his relatives. A man's relatives may also, by their conversation and questions, suggest to the dying person that he or she tell them about their condition. Quite often a dying non-Christian asks for Baptism before dying. In Christian families, the dying person may ask for the priest to be informed so that he or she may receive the sacrament of the Anointing of the Sick.

The death-bed of a father of a family is the focus of a good deal of ceremony. When he realizes that his condition is serious, the father summons all the members of family, who may come from far and wide. Only when he is surrounded by his family does he announce his successor and determine how his property is to be divided among his children so that each receives a fair share. If he has no grown-up children, he commissions one of his relatives to look after his children and their mother. He admonishes all to be attentive to their duty, and in particular to respect the ties

[70] See also J.S. Pobee, *Toward an African Theology*, 93.

126

which bind them to other clans and to the wider community of the tribe.

It is particularly important for the dying person to make good any unfulfilled promises or agreements and to arrange for the payment of debts. Because the living and the dead form one community, a person who has been untrue to his or her obligations cannot look forward to happiness either here or hereafter.

When everything has been satisfactorily settled, the dying person exhorts the assembly not to forget him or her but to remember them, along with other forebears, in the ancestral cult. If the person is a Christian, he or she asks those present for prayers. The dying person sends greetings to all who are unable to be present, and offers the last farewell: "Farewell, I am going to our own". A Christian will speak of God and pray with those present until he or she falls asleep.

It is evident that the idea of solidarity with the community, both seen and unseen, is of great importance to a dying person's peace of mind. Christian liturgy should make use of the rich African tradition, adapted of course to the demands of the faith. In many countries a start has already been made in this direction. It is good to see, for example, that the administration of the sacrament of the Anointing of the Sick is often turned into a community liturgy, instead of being treated as a private affair between the priest and the sick person. This is of course in accordance with the words of the letter of St James; "Is any among you sick? Let him call for the elders of the church, and let them pray over him, anointing him with oil in the name of the Lord; and the prayer of faith will save the sick man, and the Lord will raise him up; and if he has committed sins, he will be forgiven" (James 5:14-15).

In sickness and in death, as well as in life and strength, the Christian should have the sense of belonging to the community of faith.[71]

Clan and family solidarity persists after the burial, for people do not abandon the bereaved. The clan may appoint someone especially to offer comfort and support, perhaps by taking up residence with the family for as long as a year, until the pain of

[71] See B. Fraling, Euthanasie? Möglichkeiten und Grenzen christlicher Sterbehilfe, in: *Theologie und Glaube* 66 (1976) 408f.

127

separation has eased. In Christian communities, Masses celebrated for the dead always include prayers for the comfort of those left behind. Such Masses may be said at the request of the Christian community, beyond the immediate family, to indicate to the mourners that they are not alone.

These are wholesome traditions. There is however today a danger that Africa will be sucked into a false world where these traditions will be abandoned in favour of technical solutions to the problem of death.

3. The Danger of Uncritical Imitation of the West

The establishment of Western-type hospitals in Africa has been a mixed blessing. In Africa too now, people die in intensive care units far from family and friends. Governments, churches and medical faculties should make every effort to counteract the undesirable aspects of the new "hospital culture".

Of course Africa welcomes medical progress. In the midst of all the inevitable and often necessary modernization, however, Africa must not lose sight of its sound traditions. At the academic level, research into traditional African medicine is needed.

Hospitals should encourage a member of the family to remain in the hospital with the patient to relieve the sense of isolation and alienation. Visiting hours should be flexible, to suit relatives who may travel long distances. At the same time, patients should not be overwhelmed with visitors. It cannot help patients to recover if they are perpetually surrounded by chattering relatives. On the other hand if there is no possibility of recovery, hospital authorities should do what they can to help patients to go home to die. At university level it is absolutely necessary that medical students be taught about the traditional art of healing. They should know the traditional medicinal herbs.

During their training doctors should also receive instruction on how to deal with the dying in an African way. They too, as well as students of theology, need instruction in African religion and philosophy. This applies of course also to the nursing staff, who are usually in closer contact with the patient than is the doctor.

128

4. Final Considerations

The problem of death must be dealt with within the framework of the African tradition, which however can very easily be accommodated within the Christian vision. The African idea of a community which includes both the living and the dead is clearly very close to the Christian tradition of the communion of saints, even if the idea of the ancestors goes beyond that concept. The whole of this study has shown how close to African thought is the Christian idea of a Mystical Body, and how African theology, rooted in the concept of the ancestors, can readily develop a truly incarnated Christology and ecclesiology.

Our reflections on African attitudes to death make it plain that an important task facing African theologians is to work out an African eschatology. Africans, who live in close communion with their ancestors, should not think that becoming a Christian means abandoning the ancestors. Christ died for the virtuous ancestors too, and they live in communion with him, Proto-Ancestor and source of life. Biological life comes to us directly from our ancestors. But our real life, the life of the spirit, comes to us through Jesus Christ, who is for us grace and truth (John 1:17). An African Christian eschatology should offer people solace and strength in sickness and death, while allowing them to retain their his traditional conceptions. Pilgrims setting out on the final journey should know that they can reach their destination only by the power of God who saves through Jesus Christ. They should know too that their hope of living on in the memory of those who remain on earth is realized in the Christian community of faith united with Jesus Christ forever in prayer and in the Eucharist.

EPILOGUE

I have tried to show that African religion is essentially liberating, and that any modern African Christian theology must therefore also have as its goal the liberation of men and women.

I am not speaking of some sociopolitical liberation to be achieved through revolution, but of liberation in all its aspects, personal as well as social. People should enjoy fullness of life at every level.

It is important to observe what was laid down by the ancestors. In repeating the words and deeds of the ancestors, however, people are shaping a new tradition, transcending and completing the old by uncovering its previously unsuspected depths. Hence the future that is fashioned is much more than a copy of the past. Another example from the Bahema can illustrate this. There is a taboo on marriage between members of certain clans, but in fact such marriages do take place, in spite of the taboo, and a new tradition is in this way established. It is somewhat in this way that the memorial of the death and resurrection of Jesus can be critically integrated into the African tradition. This phenomenon of an evolving tradition may perhaps be characterized as spiral thinking, but certainly not as circular thinking.

To restore the liberating dimension of African religion, we need to rediscover some basic elements which have been buried under the combined weight of colonialism, missionary proselytism and modern technical culture. The balance of African culture has been profoundly disturbed, and many Africans know virtually nothing of their traditions, however much they may continue to be unconsciously influenced by them.

The African theologian who wishes to confront the modern challenge must be prepared to call into question the whole of his or her foreign education, and seek to construct a truly incarnated Christianity which will take equally into account both the old tradition and the demands of the modern situation. It is in that spirit that I offer this study.

A SELECTION OF BOOKS AND PERIODICALS FOR FURTHER STUDIES IN AFRICAN THEOLOGY

I. Periodicals

Africa Theological Journal, Usa River/Tanzania

African Christian Studies, Nairobi/Kenya

African Ecclesial Review (AFER), Eldoret/Kenya

Anthropos. Internationale Zeitschrift für Völker- und Sprachen- kunde, St Augustin/Bonn

Au Coeur de l'Afrique (ACA), Bujumbura/Burundi

Bulletin de Théologie Africaine (BTA), Kinshasa/Zaire

Cahiers des Religions Africaines (CRA), Kinshasa/Zaire

Evangelische Missionsmagazin, Basel u.a.

Evangelische Missionszeitschrift, Stuttgart

Journal of Theology for Southern Africa, Cape/South Africa

Missionalia, Pretoria/South Africa

Neue Zeitschrift für Missionswissenschaft (NZM), Immensee

Présence Africaine, Paris

Revue Africaine de Théologie (RAT), Kinshasa/Zaire

Revue du Clergé Africain (RCA), Mayidi/Zaire 1946-1972

Savanes-Forêts. Bulletin de Theologie et de Catéchèse, Abidjan/Ivory Coast

Spearhead, Eldoret/Kenya

Spiritus, Paris

TCNN Research Bulletin, Bukuru/Nigeria

Telema. Revue de réflexion et créativité chrétiennes en Afrique, Kinshasa/Zaire

Theologie im Kontext. Information über theologische Beiträge aus Afrika, Asien, Ozeanien und Lateinamerika, Aachen

Verbum SVD, Rome

Zeitschrift für Mission (ZM), Stuttgart

Zeitschrift für Missionswissenschaft und Religionswissenschaft, (ZMR) Münster

II. Bibliography

Adimou, C., Vodù et christianisme, in: Bulletin "Secretariatus pro non christianis" 28/29 (1975) X/1, 29-39

Adoukonou, B., Jalons pour une théologie africaine. Essai d'une herméneutique chrétienne du Vodun dahoméen, 2 vols, Paris/ Namur 1980

Adoukonou, B., Le chrétien et les moyens traditionnels de protection de la vie, in: Savanes-Forêts 3 (1981) 43-49

L'Afrique et ses formes de vie spirituelle. Actes du deuxième Colloque International de Kinshasa du 21-27 février 1983, Kinshasa 1984

Appiah-Kubi, K./Torres, S.(Eds.), African Theology en Route. Pan African Conference of Third World Theologians, New York 1979

Baëta, C. G., Christianity in Tropical Africa, London 1968

Balandier, G., The Sociology of Black Africa, New York 1970

Beti, M., The Poor Christ of Bomba, London 1971

Bimwenyi-Kweshi, O., Discours théologique négro-africain. Problème des fondements, Paris 1981. (German: Alle Dinge erzählen von Gott. Grundlegung afrikanischer Theologie, Freiburg/Basel/Wien 1982)

Boccessimo, R., Il culto dei defunti practicato dagli Acioli dell' Uganda, in: Annali del Pontifico Museo Missionario Etnologico 37 (1973) 9-62

Boesak, A., Farewell to Innocence, New York 1977

Boesak, A., Gerechtigkeit erhöht ein Volk. Texte aus dem Widerstand, Neukirchen-Vluyn 1985

Boka di Mpasi Londi, Le mariage prend le maquis, in: Telema 15 (1978) 3-4

Boka di Mpasi Londi, Inculturation chrétienne du mariage, in: Telema 17 (1979) 3-4

Buakasa-Tulu-Kia-Mpansu, L'impact de la religion africaine sur l'Afrique d'aujourd'hui: Latence et patience, in: Religions africaines et christianisme, Vol. 2, 20-32

Buakasa-Tulu-Kia-Mpansu, L'impensé du discours. "Kindoki" et "nkisi" en pays kongo au Zaire, Kinshasa ^{2}1980

Bühlmann, W., Afrika. Die Kirche unter den Völkern, Mainz 1963

Bühlmann, W., Wo der Glaube lebt, Freiburg i. Br. 1974

Bühlmann, W., Wenn Gott zu allen Menschen geht, Freiburg i. Br. 1981

Bühlmann, W., The Coming of the Third Church, London 1976

Bühlmann, W., The Missions on Trial: a moral for the future from the archives of today, London 1978

Bühlmann, W., Wenn Gott zu allen Menschen geht, Freiburg i. Br. 1981

Bühlmann, W., Fragen zu Ehe und Familie. Bringt 'Familiaris Consortio' die Antwort?, in: ThdG 25 (1982) 159-171

Bühlmann, W., The Church of the Future: a Model for the Year 2001, London 1986

Bühlmann, W., With Eyes to See: Church and World in the Third Millenium, New York 1990

Bujo, B., Kultur und Christentum in Afrika. Bemerkungen zu einem Aufsatz, in: NZM 32 (1976) 212-216

Bujo, B., Afrikanische Theologie. Rückblick auf eine Kontroverse, in: ZMR 61 (1977) 118-127

Bujo, B., Der afrikanische Ahnenkult und die christliche Verkündigung, in: ZMR 64 (1980) 293-306; or: Nos ancêtres, ces saints inconnus, in: Bulletin de Théologie Africaine 1 (1979) 165-178

Bujo, B., Les ordres religieux de l'époque post-coloniale en Afrique. Espérance ou déception?, in: CRA 14 (1980) 141-150

Bujo, B., African Morality and Christian faith, in: African Christian Morality at the Age of Inculturation, Nairobi 1990, 39-72

Bujo, B., Notes complémentaires à la contribution sur le mariage africain et chrétien, in: Combats pour un christianisme africain, 45-49

Bujo, B., Déchristianiser en christianisant? in: BTA 4 (1982) 229-242

Bujo, B., What Kind of Theology Does Africa Need? Inculturation Alone is not enough, in: African Christian Morality at the Age of Inculturation, Nairobi 1990, 119-130

Bujo, B., Au nom de l'évangile. Refus d'un christianisme néocolonialiste, in: BTA 6 (1984) 117-127

Bujo, B., Die pastoral-ethische Beurteilung der Polygamie in Afrika, in: FZPhTh 31 (1984) 177-189; summarized as: Polygamy in Africa: A Pastoral Approach, in: Theology Digest 32 (1985) 230-234

Bujo, B., African Morality: Individual Responsibility and Communitarian Dimension, in: African Christian Morality at the Age of Inculturation, Nairobi 1990, 95-102

Bujo, B., Comment être religieux en Afrique aujourd'hui?, in: Select 18 (1985) 13-16

Bujo, B., L'apport africain à une conception de l'Eglise, in: Sources/Fribourg 11 (1985) 250-257

Bujo, B., Can Morality be Christian in Africa, in: African Christian Studies 4 (1988) 5-39

Bujo, B., Do we still need the ten commandments?, Nairobi 1990

Bujo, B., "Des prêtres noirs s'interrogent". Une théologie issue de la négritude?, in: NZM 46 (1990) 286-297

Bujo, B., Auf der Suche nach einer afrikanischen Christologie, in: Dembowski, H./ Greive, W. (Eds.), Der andere Christus. Christologie in Zeugnissen aus aller Welt, Erlangen 1991, 87-99

Bujo, B., La remise en question du discours traditionnel en morale face à un monde polycentrique, in: Pinto de Oliveira, C. J. (Ed.), Novitas et Veritas Vitae. Aux sources du renouveau de la morale chrétienne, (Mélanges S. Pinckaers), Fribourg 1991, 161-173

Bukasa, J. et alii, Chemins de la christologie africaine, Paris 1986

Césaire, A., Cahier d'un retour au pays natal, Paris 1933

Césaire, A., Une Saison au Congo, Paris 1966

Coco, D., Notes sur la place des morts et des ancêtres dans la société traditionnelle (Fou, Gen, Yoruba du Bas-Dahomey), in: Les religions africaines comme source des valeurs de civilisation. Colloque de Cotonou (16-22 août 1970), Paris 1972, 226-237

134

Combats pour un christianisme africain (Mélanges V. Mulago), Collection, Kinshasa 1981

Damman, E., Die Religionen Afrikas, Stuttgart 1963; (or Les Religions de l'Afrique, Paris 1978)

De Haes, R., Recherches africaines sur le mariage chrétien, in: Combats pour un christianisme africain, 33-43

Dickson, K.A./Ellingworth, P.(Eds.), Theology in Africa, London/New York 1984

Des prêtres noirs s'interrogent, Collection, Bruxelles 1956

Ditona-Di-Lelo, Afrique et Evangélisation. Recherche d'une identité chrétienne propre (Diss.), Rome 1987

Eboussi-Boulaga, F., Métamorphoses africaines, in: Christus 20 (1973) 29-39

Eboussi-Boulaga, F., La crise du Muntu. Authenticité africaine et philosophie, Paris 1977

Eboussi-Boulaga, F., Christianity without Fetishes. An African Critique and Recapture of Christianity, Maryknoll (New York) 1984

Ela, J. M., Ancestors and Christian Faith: An African Problem, Concilium 102 (1977) 34-50

Ela, J. M., African Cry, New York 1986

Ela, J. My Faith as an African, Maryknoll (N.Y.) 1988

Ela, J. M./Luneau, R., Voici le temps des héritiers, Paris 1981

Fabella, V./ Oduyoye, M.A. (Eds.), With Passion and Compassion. Third World Women Doing Theology, Maryknoll (N.Y.) 1988, 3-65

Fanon, F., The Wretched of the Earth, New York 1968

Fiedler, K., Christentum und afrikanische Kultur. Konservative deutsche Missionare in Tanzania 1900-1940, Gütersloh 1983

Frostin, P., Liberation Theology in Tanzania and South Africa. A First World Interpretation, Malmö 1988

Furger, F., Inkulturation - eine Herausforderung an die Moraltheologie. Bestandsaufnahme und methodologische Rückfragen, in: NZM 40 (1984) 177-193; 241-258

135

Goba, B., Jésus Christ mort pour nos péchés, ressuscité pour notre vie, in: Spiritus 90 (1983) 55-62

Gravrand, H., La prière sérèer. Expérience et language religieux, in: Religions africaines et christianisme, vol. 1., 105-125

Griaule, M., Dieu d'eau, Paris 1948

Guariglia, G., L'Etre Suprême, le culte des ancêtres et le sacrifice expiatoire chez les Igbo du sud-est Nigéria, in: CRA 4 (1970) 244-246

Häselbarth, H., Die Auferstehung der Toten in Afrika. Eine theologische Deutung der Todesriten der Mamabolo in Nordtransvaal, Gütersloh 1972

Hastings, A., Christian Marriage in Africa, London 1973

Haule, C., Bantu "Witchcraft" and Christian Morality, Schöneck-Beckenried 1969

Hertlein, S., Wege christlicher Verkündigung, 2 vols. in 3, Münsterschwarzach 1976/1983

Hillman, E., Polygamy Reconsidered, New York 1975

Idowu, Bolaji E., African Traditional Religion. A Definition, London 1973

Imfeld, A., Verlernen, was mich stumm macht. Lesebuch zur afrikanischen Kultur, Zürich 1980

Inculturation et libération en Afrique aujourd'hui. Mélanges en l'honneur du Prof. Mulago gwa Cikala (Collectif), Kinshasa 1990

Kairos Theologians - challenge to the Church (Gweru, Zimbabwe 1985)

Kamainda, Th., "Deux conceptions monothéistes dans l'Uele", in: Approche du non-chrétien. Rapports et compte-rendu de la XXXIVe Semaine de Missiologie, Louvain 1964, 45-55

Kanyamachumbi, P., Réflexion théologique sur la religion des ancêtres en Afrique Centrale, in: RCA 24 (1969) 421-455

Kayoya, M., My Father's Footprints, Nairobi 1973

Kesteloot, L., Négritude et situation coloniale, Yaoundé 1970

Kisembo, B./Magesa, L./Shorter, A., African Christian Marriage, London 1977

136

Ki-Zerbo, J., Histoire de l'Afrique, Paris 1972. (German: Die Geschichte Schwarz-Afrikas, Wuppertal 1981)

Köster, F., Afrikanisches Christsein, Einsiedeln 1977

Kollbrunner, F., Auf dem Weg zu einer christlichen Ahnenverehrung?, in: NZM 31 (1975) 19-29; 110-123

Laleyé, I. P., La personnalité africaine. Pierres d'attente pour une société globale, in: Combats pour un christianisme africain, 137-147

Legrain, M., Mariage chrétien, modèle unique? Questions venues d'Afrique, Paris 1978

Lobinger, F., Katechisten als Gemeindeleiter: Dauereinrichtung oder Übergangslösung? Erfahrungen in der Afrikamission, Münsterschwarzach 1973

Losigo-Kulu, A., Perspectives ecclésiologiques en Afrique francophone. Pour une théologie de l'Eglise locale à la lumière du Synode de 1974 (Diss.), Rome 1991

Lufuluabo, F. M., Mariage coutumier et mariage chrétien indissoluble, Kinshasa 1969

Mandefu-Kambuyi, B., L'impact d'un discours anthropo-théocentrique sur les communautés ecclésiales vivantes. L'enjeu d'une nouvelle manière d'être Eglise (Diss.), Rome 1990

Mariama Bâ, Ein so langer Brief. Ein afrikanisches Frauenschicksal, Wuppertal 1980

Mawinza, J., Specific Difference between the Attitude toward the Ancestral Spirits and Worship of God, in: CRA 3 (1969) 37-47

Mbiti, J. S., Afrikanische Beiträge zur Christologie, in: Beyerhaus, P./Gensichen, H.W./Rosenkranz, G./Vicedom, G.(Eds.), Theologische Stimmen aus Asien, Afrika und Lateinamerika, vol. 3, München 1968, 72-85

Mbiti, J. S., L'eschatologie, in: Dickson, K.A./Ellingworth, P. (Eds.), Pour une théologie africaine, 219-253

Mbiti, J. S., Concepts of God in Africa, London 1970

Mbiti, J. S., New Testament Eschatology in an African Background. A Study of Encounter between New Testament and African Traditional Concepts, London 1971

Mbiti, J. S., Some African Concepts of Christology, in: Vicedom, G. (Ed.), Christ and the Younger Churches, London 1972, 51-62

Mbiti, J. S., An Introduction to African Religion, London 1975

Mbiti, J. S., African Religions and Philosophy, London 1983

Mbonyinkebe-Sebahire, Brèves réflexions sur la conception traditionnelle du péché en Afrique Centrale, in: CRA 8 (1974) 155-165

Mitima, E., La place de l'intention dans l'acte moral chez les Bantu (Unpublished thesis for the licenciate), Kinshasa 1980

Mort, funérailles, deuil et le culte des ancêtres chez les populations du Kwango/Bas-Kwilu. Rapports et compte-rendu de la IIIe Semaine d'Etudes Ethno-Pastorales (Bandundu 1967), Bandundu 1969

Mpongo, L., Le mariage chrétien en afrique noire. A propos d'un article, in: Orientations Pastorales 120 (1968) 313-333

Mpongo, L., L'infécondité comme empêchement dirimant?, in: RCA 24 (1969) 696-711

Mpongo, L., La liturgie du mariage dans la perspective africaine, in: La mariage chrétien en Afrique (Ve Semaine Théologique de Kinshasa), Mayidi 1971, 175-197

Mugambi, J.N.K. / Magesa, L. (Eds.), Jesus in African Christianity Experimentation and Diversity in African Christology, Nairobi 1989

Mugambi, J.N.K. / Magesa, L. (Eds.), The Church in African Christianity. Innovative Essays in Ecclesiology, Nairobi 1990

Mujynya, E.N., Le mystère de la mort dans le monde bantu, in: CRA 3 (1969) 25-35; 199-208

Mujynya, E.N., Le mal et le fondement dernier de la morale chez les Bantu interlacustres, in: CRA 3 (1969) 55-78

Mujynya, E.N., L'homme dans l'univers des Bantu, Lubumbashi 1972

Mulago, V., Le pact du sang et le sacrifice comme symboles pour la communion eucharistique, In: Des prêtres noirs s'interrogent

Mulago, V., Un visage africain du christianisme. L'union vitale bantu face à l'unité vitale ecclésiale, Paris 1965

Mulago, V., La conception de Dieu dans la tradition bantoue, in: RCA 22 (1967) 272-299

Mulago, V., Die lebensnotwendige Teilhabe, in: Bürkle, H. (Ed.)
Theologie und Kirche in Afrika, Stuttgart 1968, 54-72

Mulago, V., Le Dieu des Bantu, in: CRA 2 (1968) 23-64

Mulago, V., Le problème d'une Théologie africaine revue à la lumière
de Vatican II, in: RCA 24 (1969) 277-314

Mulago, V., Symbolisme dans les religions traditionnelles africaines et
sacramentalisme, in: RCA 27 (1972) 467-502

Mulago, V., Eléments fondamentaux de la religion africaine, in
Religions africaines et christianisme, vol. 1, 45-49

Mulago, V., La religion traditionnelle des Bantu et leur vision du
monde, Kinshasa 1980

Mulago, Gwa Cikala Musharhamina, Traditional African Marriage and
Christian Marriage, Kampala 1983

Museka-Ntumba, L., La nomination africaine de Jésus Christ. Quelle
Christologie? (Diss.), Louvain-la-Neuve 1988

Mutiso-Mubinda, Anthropology and the Paschal Mystery (Spearhead),
Eldoret/Kenya 1979

Mveng, E., Les sources grecques de l'histoire négro-africaine depuis
Homère jusqu'à Strabon, Paris 1972

Mveng, E., Christ as Master of Initiation, in: Study Encounter 9 (1973)
3-5

Mveng, E., Essai d'anthropologie négro-africaine: La personne
humaine, in: Religions africaines et christianisme, vol. 2, 85-96

Mveng, E., Spiritualité africaine et spiritualité chrétienne, in: L'Afrique
et ses formes de vie spirituelle, 263-279

Mwene-Batende, Mouvements messianiques et protestation sociale. Le
cas du Kitawala chez les Kumu du Zaïre, Kinshasa 1982

Neckebrouck, V., Le onzième commandement. Etiologie d'une église
indépendante au pied du mont Kenya, Immensee 1981

Ngindu, A., Unité et pluralité de la théologie, in: RCA 22 (1967)
593-615

Ngindu, A., The History of Theology in Africa. From Polemics to
Critical Irenics, in: Appiah-Kubi, K./Torres, S. (Eds.), African Theology

en Route. Pan African Conference of Third World Theologians, New York 1979, 23-35

Ngugi wa Thiong'o, Devil on the Cross, Nairobi 1984

Nothomb, D., Un humanisme africain. Valeurs et pierres d'attente, Bruxelles 1965

Ntetem, M., Die negro-afrikanische Stammesinitiation. Religionsgeschichtliche Darstellung. Theologische Wertung, Möglichkeit der Christianisierung, Münsterschwarzach 1983

Nyamiti, C., New Theologicial Approach. A New Vision of the Church in Africa, in: RAT 2 (1978) 33-53

Nyamiti, C., Christ's Resurrection in the Light of African Tribal Initiation Ritual, in: RAT 3 (1979) 171-184

Nyamiti, C., Christ as Our Ancestor. Christology from an African Perspective, Gweru/Zimbabwe 1984

Nyamiti, C., The Mass as Divine and Ancestoral Encounter between the Living and the Dead, in: African Christian Studies 1 (1985) 28-48

Nyeme-Tese, A., Ethique en un milieu africain, Ingenbohl 1974

Oduyoye, M.A., Hearing and Knowing. Theological Reflections on Christianity in Africa, Maryknoll (N.Y.) 1986

Okot p'Bitek, The Song of Lawino, New York 1969/Nairobi 1972

Pauwels, M., Usages funèbres au Ruanda, in: Anthropos 48 (1953) 30-43

Penoukou, E.J., Réalité africaine et salut en Jésus-Christ, in: Spiritus 89 (1982) 374-392

Pilo, K., La sociologie des institutions matrimoniales chez les Bahema (Unpublished dissertation), Rome 1982

Pobee, J.S., Toward an African Theology, Nashville 1979

Pöllitzer, Ph., Ancestor Veneration in the Oruuano Movement, in: Missionalia 12 (1984) 124-128

Pour un Concile africain. Documents du Colloque d'Abidjan: Civilisation noire et Eglise Catholique (1977), Paris 1978

140

Reisach, Ch., Das Wort und seine Macht in Afrika. Probleme der Kommunikation und Information für die Verkündigung, Münsterschwarzach 1981

Religions africaines et christianisme. Colloque international de Kinshasa (1978), 2 vols., Kinshasa 1979

Renouveau de l'Eglise et nouvelles églises, collection, Mayidi 1969

Rivinius, K.J. (Ed.), Schuld, Sühne und Erlösung in Zentralafrika (Zaïre) und in der christlichen Theologie Europas, St. Augustin 1983

Rücker, H., "Afrikanische Theologie". Darstellung und Dialog, Innsbruck/Wien 1985

Ruytinx, J., La morale bantoue et le problème de l'éducation morale au Congo, Bruxelles 1960

Sanon, A. T., Tierce Eglise, Ma Mère. La conversion d'une communauté païenne au Christ, Bobo/Dioulasso 1977

Sanon, A. T., & R. Luneau: Enraciner l'évangile. Initiations africaines et pédagogie de la foi, Paris 1982. (German: Das Evangelium verwurzeln. Glaubenserschließung im Raum afrikanischer Stammesinitiationen, Freiburg/Basel/Wien 1985)

Sawyerr, H., Grundlagen einer Theologie für Afrika, in: Gensichen, H.W./Rosenkranz, G./Vicedom, G.(Eds.), Theologische Stimmen aus Asien, Afrika und Lateinamerika, vol. 1, München 1965, 110-126

Sawyerr, H., Creative Evangelism. Towards a New Christian Encounter with Africa, London 1968

Sawyerr, H., What is African Theology?, in: African Theological Journal 4 (1971) 7-24

Schebesta, P., My Pygmy and Negro Hosts, vol. 1, London 1936

Schebesta, P., Revisiting my Pygmy Hosts, vol. 2, London 1936

Schreiter, R.J. (Ed.), Faces of Jesus in Africa, New York 1991

Senghor, L.S., Négritude und Humanismus, Düsseldorf 1967

Senghor, L.S., Eléments constructifs d'une civilisation d'inspiration négro-africaine, in: Présence Africaine 24-25 (1959) 249-279

Setiloane, G., Theological Trends in Africa, in: Missionalia 8 (1980) 47-53

Smet, A.J., La Jamaa dans l'oeuvre du Père Placide Tempels, in: Religions africaines et christianisme, vol. 1, 265-269

Sundermeier, Th. (Ed.), Christus, der schwarze Befreier, Erlangen 1973

Sundermeier, Th. (Ed.), Zwischen Kultur und Politik. Texte zur afrikanischen und zur schwarzen Theologie, Hamburg 1978

Tempels, Pl., Bantu philosophy, Paris 1959

Tempels, Pl., Catéchèse bantoue, in: Le Bulletin des Missions 22 (1948) 258-279

Tempels, Pl., Notre rencontre, 2 vol., Limete/Leopoldville (Zaïre) 1962

Théologie africaine. Bilan et perspectives. Actes de la Dix- septième Semaine Théologique de Kinshasa (Collectif), Kinshasa 1989

Theuws, J., Death and burial in Africa, in: Concilium 32 (1968) 140-143

Thiel, J. F., Die übermenschlichen Wesen bei Yansi und einigen ihrer Nachbarn (Zaïre), in: Anthropos (1972) 649-689

Thiel, J. F., Ahnen, Geister, Höchste Wesen, St. Augustin 1977

Tshibangu, Th., Vers une théologie de couleur africaine?, in: RCA 15 (1960) 333-346

Tshibangu, Th., Le propos d'une théologie africaine, Kinshasa 1974

Tutu, D., Versöhnung ist unteilbar. Biblische Interpretationen zur Schwarzen Theologie. [With an autobiography of the author] Wuppertal 1985

Umezinwa, W.A., La religion dans la littérature africaine, Kinshasa 1975

Umezinwa, W.A., The Idiom of Plastic Figures in Chinua Achebe's Novels, in: Religions africaines et christianisme, vol. 2, 125- 133

Upkong, J.S., The Emergence of African Theologies, in: Theological Studies 45 (1984) 501-536

Uzukwu, E.E., Le salut chrétien du point de vue congolais, in: Spiritus 89 (1982) 247-267

Vers le Synode Africain, in: Concilium, Cahier spécial, n. 239, 1992

Vandenberghe, D., Contribution à la pastorale du mariage en Afrique, in: Orientations Pastorales 119 (1968) 221-254

Vanneste, A., Une Faculté de Théologie en Afrique, in: RCA 13 (1958) 225-236

Vanneste, A., D'abord une vraie théologie, in: RCA 15 (1960) 346-352

Vanneste, A., Théologie universelle et Théologie africaine, in: RCA 24 (1969) 324-336

Vanneste, A., Où en est le problème de la théologie africaine?, in: Cultures et Développement 6 (1974) 149-167

Waldenfels, H. (Ed.), Theologen der Dritten Welt. Elf biographische Skizzen aus Afrika, Asien und Lateinamerika, München 1982

Wiedenmann, L. (Ed.), Herausgefordert durch die Armen. Dokumente der Ökumenischen Vereinigung von Dritte-Welt-Theologen 1976-1983, Freiburg/Basel/Wien 1983